ReGENERATION

A MANIFESTO FOR AMERICA'S NEXT LEADERS

Rebecca Ryan

Spring is coming!

Rebecca

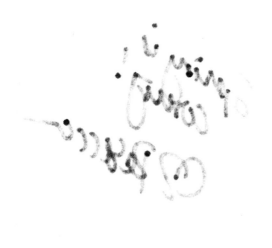

ReGENERATION

Copyright 2013 by Rebecca Ryan

Printed and bound in the United States of America by Omnipress.

First Printing Date: June 2013 by Next Generation Consulting®

ISBN-10: 0977874672

ISBN-13: 978-0-9778746-7-5

Inquiries regarding permission for use of the materials contained in this book should be directed to Rebecca Ryan.

On the web: www.nextgenerationconsulting.com

By email: info@nextgenerationconsulting.com

Call toll-free: 888-922-9596

By snail mail: Next Generation Consulting

211 S. Paterson, Suite 280

Madison, WI 53703 USA

Orders: www.nextgenerationconsulting.com

Kindle Bookstore

iBookstore

Dedication

This book is dedicated to the great-great-grandchildren

of my godson, Avery Joseph Faul.

CONTENTS

I wrote this book because I want a better country. For all of us. And I know a lot of you do, too.

We want a better country because we know deep in our guts that what we're doing isn't working. We want a better country because we worry that our kids and grandkids aren't going to have it as good as we did. We want a better country because we sense that the folks in Washington are out of touch and incapable of getting things done.

We know the rich are getting richer, the poor are getting poorer, and the middle class? It's evaporating. We wonder what "the American dream" means anymore, or if it even exists.

We want a better country because at this rate, reality TV is the only thing we'll have to show for the first part of the 21st century.

We can do so much better.

I wrote this book because I believe that America is going through a period of decline that will last through about 2020. I call this period "winter." And if you've ever experienced winter, you know that things seem to die. But they don't; they hibernate. Squirrels, birds, trees, Packers fans[1]—they all take a nice long rest during winter.

---

1   I was born in Green Bay and have to give a shout-out to my peeps. Go, Pack! (This is probably also a good time to let you know that I use footnotes to cite sources, and sometimes to offer a bit of additional commentary.) Thanks for joining me on the ride.

Winter's not forever. Spring will come again. And between now and then lies a magical period—a period of regeneration during which we'll face decisions about what kind of country we are, and what we want to leave for our children, and theirs.

This book is for the change agents, the up-and-comers, our wise elders, social entrepreneurs, and anyone willing to rethink and reshape America.

This book is for everyone who senses that what we're doing isn't working, and is hell-bent on reinventing an America that works better for more people.

We can rock this. Let's get started.

Rebecca Ryan

Madison, Wisconsin

June 2013

There is a mysterious cycle in human events.

To some generations much is given.

Of other generations much is expected.

This generation of Americans has a rendezvous with destiny.

Franklin D. Roosevelt, 1936

PART ONE: WINTER IN AMERICA

Wherever you live in America, you experience seasons. They are regular and predictable, nature's rhythm of birth, maturation, aging, and death.

I have lived in the American Midwest for long stretches of my life, and am comforted by the region's four distinct seasons.[2]

In the spring, I enjoy watching my neighbors emerge from their homes to aerate their lawns or seed their gardens. They're usually a little pudgy and pale after their winter hibernation—afternoons spent watching football games and indulging in rich, gravy-laden crockpot dinners. By April after the daffodils have broken through, I start to sleep with the windows open and literally wake up with the birds, who begin to bicker loudly in my neighbor Sandy's tree before daybreak.

The university students vacate by mid-May and won't be back again until August. While they're gone, the weather turns glorious and work slows down. It's a treat to skip out early and meet friends at Lake Mendota, where we putter about on a boat talking smart and sometimes pretending to fish. It's 8:30 before the sun sets, the dog days of summer.

In September, our weekends are gobbled up, canning and preserving the last of the summer's harvest—pickles, tomatoes, beans. The days grow shorter, and the leaves in our neighborhood turn too quickly from dark green to yellow and then to orange and deep red. Then, on one dreadful day—usually in November—we finally give in; it's time to turn on the heat.

---

2   I currently live in Madison, Wisconsin, where the university's academic cycle further punctuates each year's seasons.

Winter in Wisconsin...

Winter is an acquired taste. With its short days and long nights, it seems there's never enough daylight to get everything done. I fall asleep before nine, sometimes as early as seven. And then there's the snow, which I love—inches of it. A blanket to cover the earth while she sleeps. Winter is a time of hibernation, when living things go dormant to store up their energy and rest... to prepare for the next spring.

Figure 1: Seasons in America

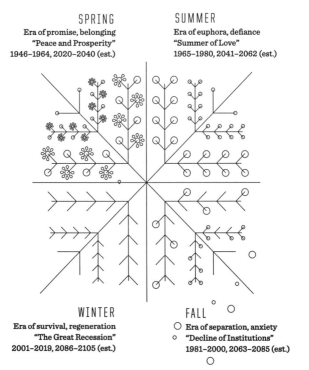

SPRING
Era of promise, belonging
"Peace and Prosperity"
1946–1964, 2020–2040 (est.)

SUMMER
Era of euphora, defiance
"Summer of Love"
1965–1980, 2041–2062 (est.)

WINTER
Era of survival, regeneration
"The Great Recession"
2001–2019, 2086–2105 (est.)

FALL
Era of separation, anxiety
"Decline of Institutions"
1981–2000, 2063–2085 (est.)

Seasons are nature's cycle of regeneration, a reminder that there's an order to things, there are things that are larger than me. Larger than you.

American life and society cycle through seasons, too.[3] They're as predictable as nature's, but each season lasts, on average, 20 years, so you and I rarely live long enough to endure a whole cycle. Here's what America's seasons are like:

America started during a winter period (the American Revolution), and our country has completed three entire spring-summer-fall-winter cycles in the last 200-plus years. We're in our fourth winter now.

To enliven this concept of America's "seasons," here's a quick recap of our most recent cycle. As you read the following paragraphs, can you see yourself, your parents, your grandparents, your children, your community taking shape in these seasons?

---

3   Authors Neil Howe and William Strauss introduced the concept of American "seasons" in their book, *The Fourth Turning* (New York: Broadway Books, 1997).

» *Spring* came to America on the heels of the allies' World War II victory and lasted from 1946 to 1964. Twelve million vets, most members of the GI Generation (b. 1901–1925), came home from the war, birthed the Baby Boomers (b. 1946–1964), and took advantage of the GI Bill: low-cost mortgages, loans to start a business or farm, cash payments of tuition and living expenses to attend college, high school, or vocational education, and one year of unemployment compensation.

The economy responded—like a rocket. Incomes nearly doubled, from $3,940 per year in 1946 to $6,900 in 1960. Innovations like lightweight furniture, washing machines, and vacuum cleaners transformed daily life, and—coupled with those higher incomes—allowed more Americans to reach the middle class and enjoy amenities that had once been reserved for the wealthy. By the end of the 1950s, 87 percent of all American families owned at least one TV, 75 percent owned cars, and 60 percent owned their homes.[4] This was living! President Eisenhower's 1956 reelection slogan captured the springtime mood, "Peace and Prosperity."

---

4   *Nation's Business*, vol. 48. Chamber of Commerce of the United States of America, 1960.

» *Summer,* a season of heightened consciousness, began in August 1965 when a Caucasian police officer apprehended a black man suspected of driving drunk in a Los Angeles neighborhood. That event sparked a five-day riot, pitting enraged, mostly black citizens against mostly white storeowners, who were seen as exploiting blacks by selling inferior goods for inflated prices. The Watts riots claimed 35 lives, injured 1,000 more, and destroyed 600 buildings.

The riots were a local tragedy that turned into a national crisis thanks to television, through which the story found its way into nearly every American home. The crisis sparked a renewed energy for civil rights, especially among America's youth, Baby Boomers who were in their teens and 20s.

Throughout the 1960s and 70s, Boomers staked out a new American consciousness, one rooted in freedom, equality, and love. Three major movements—civil rights, women's rights, and environmentalism—took root. Young Americans expressed themselves and their new consciousness through their clothing, music, drug use, and rebellion. They protested against the Vietnam War and stood together against what they saw as the Establishment. Bill Clinton summarized the "culture wars" that emerged during this time and the ensuing political polarization that resulted from this period:

If you look back on the Sixties and think there was more good than bad, you're probably a Democrat. If you think there was more harm than good, you're probably a Republican.[5]

Summer lasted from 1965 through about 1980, when Ronald Reagan was elected president. These are the birth years of Generation X.

» *Fall* started during Ronald Reagan's presidency, a time when hippies became yuppies and consumer culture replaced youth culture. During this period, long-standing institutions began to show signs of decay. Our sense of safety dissolved as we printed photos of missing children on milk cartons. Our trust in the US government deteriorated as the Iran-Contra scandal was exposed. Our faith in our elders was shaken when we watched the space shuttle *Challenger* explode during a live broadcast into elementary, middle school, and high school classrooms. Our confidence in our financial systems crumbled with the farm crisis and the savings and loan meltdown. And the nuclear family, the bastion of cultural norms and the familiar safety blanket for America's next generation, was shredded as divorce rates climbed. The 1979 tearjerker movie *Kramer vs. Kramer* was the too-true anthem of Generation X's family life: moms and dads filing for divorce and fighting for custody as children questioned their parents' character and loyalties.

---

5   Quoted in M. J. Heale, "The Sixties as History: A Review of the Political Historiography," *Reviews in American History* 33, no. 1 (2005): 132.

Combined, these crises shook America's sense of security. We became more fearful and individualistic. The phrase "What's in it for me?" entered the lexicon. Although the Clinton years offered a glimmer of economic hope, Americans became more divided politically and less equal economically. Fall lasted from about 1981 to 2001, the birth years of the Millennials.

> » *Winter* crashed into America when two planes hit the World Trade
> Center on September 11, 2001. Any remnants of safety and security
> we felt were blown to bits. By 2002, America's long-running bull
> market had ground to a halt. Wall Street hustled to find new ways to
> make money and prop up America's financial system. The housing
> bubble was born, preceding the economic meltdown of 2008 and
> subsequent Great Recession.

For the first time in years, America's status as an infallible superpower was in question. Stalwarts of American security crumbled. Government-backed mortgage lenders Fannie Mae and Freddie Mac went under, the economy froze, unemployment hit record highs, consumer confidence dwindled, and a highly polarized and paralyzed Congress proved incapable of negotiating its way to a jobs bill or a debt ceiling negotiation in 2011. And then there was the fiscal cliff . . .

Americans are bitterly divided on how to get out of this mess, and for many of us alive at this moment, we're still reeling. How did this happen? For as long as we can remember, the economy has been expanding, unemployment has been low, and America has been the envy of other nations. We've always had rising housing values and readily available credit.

But here's the truth, and I'm not going to sugarcoat it: those days are over for quite a while.

We have entered winter. A period when the whole country is resetting. Hibernating. Regathering. And it feels scary.

We see loved ones who've been laid off struggle to find work.

We send our soldiers back for a third—even a fourth—tour of duty. And when they finally come home, they are transformed. Damaged.

Our bankers tell us that our homes aren't worth what we paid for them; our equity has vanished.

We open our mail and see that our credit card companies have once again increased our rate . . . to 19, 20, 24 percent.

Our kids finish their college degrees—even hustle for double majors— but can't find jobs.

Boomers, who'd planned to be retired by now, are still working, afraid they won't be able to live on what they've saved.

Our grandparents, always stoic, take their medicines and skip their dinners.

Winter is brutal. We are being forced to make choices and confront realities that many of us never saw coming.

But if you can take a step back from the daily grind and look at America in a broader context, you'll see that we've been through winters before. Three of them, to be exact. They have been bitter, and often bloody. In the Civil War, more than 600,000 Americans were massacred . . . by each other. It almost makes our current winter look easy by comparison.

And each time, America has reemerged. Regathered. Regenerated.

Better.

Stronger.

All of you reading these words right now have what President Roosevelt called "a rendezvous with destiny." Spring will come again. But until then, we have a sobering agenda. The questions we ask, the responsibilities we undertake, the partnerships we enliven, the time and money we invest—all of these things will determine the quality of our coming spring.

Americans alive during this winter have a noble task: to think and work and act not for ourselves (because many of us may not be alive when spring comes again). We must act with the wisdom and grace to do our best for our children, and theirs.

This is winter's task. This is our rendezvous with destiny.

So let me pour you a glass of history, to see that we have been here before, in winter. And we have always emerged renewed. And we can again.

The Revolution was in the minds and hearts of the people ... This radical change in the principles, opinions, sentiments, and affections of the people was the real American Revolution.

John Adams, 1818

America's First Winter:

The American Revolution, 1763-1783

As you may remember from your high school history class, non-Europeans have lived in America since prehistoric times. White dudes came much later. European settlement started after Christopher Columbus's voyages in 1492. Then beginning in 1607, the English started looking at America like an Atkins dieter looks at a donut. The Brits took a serious fancy to America throughout the 1600s and 1700s, migrating here in droves. By the 1770s, the thirteen colonies[6] contained 2.5 million people. That's the population of today's San Diego.

Britain saw the American colonies as they saw everything—as an extension of the British empire. And King George III, with his bulging, wide-set eyes and powdered wig, expected the colonies to pay their loyalties to the British crown.

And by loyalties, he meant taxes.

This didn't sit well with the colonists. They felt it was unfair to pay taxes to a faraway government that wouldn't even allow them to have a seat in Parliament. If you've heard the term "taxation without representation," this is where it started.

---

6   Can you name them? In alpha order: Connecticut, Delaware, Georgia, Maryland, Massachusetts Bay, New Hampshire, New Jersey, New York, North Carolina, Pennsylvania, Rhode Island and Providence Plantations, South Carolina, and Virginia.

A pissing match ensued: King George III demanded loyalty (er, taxes), and the American "Patriots"—the term adopted by colonists who wanted to be free of England—rejected the king's demands.

By 1776, the Patriots had had enough already. They issued the *United States Declaration of Independence*, a powdered-wig version of giving the king a big, fat middle finger. This was a turning point in our country's history. The declaration told the monarchy to piss off and pronounced the United States an independent, sovereign nation.

This really made King George's eyes bulge, and you know where this goes. Boys being boys, it erupted into the American Revolutionary War, pitting the British army against the American Patriots, each side fighting for control of the United States.

The Patriots hung on by their teeth and eventually they prevailed, barely. The British troops surrendered in October 1781. In 1783, both sides signed the Treaty of Paris, which formally and finally terminated any claims the British Empire had on the United States. America was free, plunging headlong into a brave new political experiment: a republican democracy.

That's enough for the historical play-by-play. Not as good as HBO's *John Adams*, but still, pretty inspiring.

What can the American Revolution teach us about our current winter?

Three things.

{1}

For starters—and with the benefit of hindsight—the American Revolution could've been predicted. In this section's opening quote from 1818, John Adams reflected that the war was simply a response to the radical change that had already been brewing in colonists' hearts and minds.

The "radical change" was the American Enlightenment, a period marked by entirely new ways of thinking about class, politics, freedom, and tolerance.

To wrap your head around just how radical the American Enlightenment was, remember that in Britain, your class in society was mostly determined by your birth. If you were born into a land-owning class, for example, you had more rights and privileges than those who weren't. There was no "working your way up" the class system in Britain. You were sort of stuck. The ovarian lottery.

Oh! And also, in England there was one ruling church. Different religious views were forbidden.

So . . . being British was unpleasant if you weren't born into a wealthy family or if you didn't share the beliefs of the Church of England.

John Adams and our forebears saw this religious intolerance and lack of social and economic mobility as deeply unjust. They embraced the American Enlightenment's revolutionary idea that *all people are equal at birth*. We yawn at this idea now, but in its time, it was a mind-blowing, what-the-hell? idea. It ran completely counter to prevailing, traditional government and religious power structures. But it's a central principle on which our country is based, and one for which thousands of people were willing to die.

The Declaration of Independence reads: "We hold these Truths to be self-evident, that all Men are created equal, that they are endowed by their Creator with certain unalienable rights, that among these are Life, Liberty, and the pursuit of Happiness."

So the first lesson from the American Revolution is that the seeds of winter are usually planted long before the season actually arrives.[7]

{2}

The second lesson of the American Revolution is that winter often causes America to question itself, especially on matters related to freedom and equality. And generally, America comes through winter by extending *more* liberties to *more* people.

---

7   We'll see this again with the Civil War and Reconstruction; that period of winter was also predetermined by actions America took leading up to it.

In our current winter, America is once again asking the question: "Who gets America's rights and freedoms?" Do gays? Do immigrants? Do fetuses? We'll come back to these issues a bit later, but for now, just note America's wintertime tendency to question itself.

{3}

A final lesson of the American Revolution is that not all colonists bought into the idea that America should be independent from Britain. Some *liked* being British subjects. They were called "Loyalists"; they supported King George and wanted America to pay taxes to Britain and remain British property.

The differences between the Patriots who fought for American freedom and the Loyalists who fought against it are instructive. Historian Leonard Woods Labaree compared traits of the Loyalists against those of the Patriots and found that:

» Loyalists were older and better-established men than the Patriots. Many, especially merchants in the port cities, had maintained strong and long-standing relations with Britain and often had business and family links to other parts of the British Empire.

» Loyalists tended to resist innovation.

» Loyalists thought that resistance to the Crown, which they insisted was the only legitimate government, was morally wrong, while the Patriots thought morality was on their side.

» Loyalists were alienated when the Patriots resorted to violence, such as burning houses and tarring and feathering.

» Loyalists wanted to take a centrist position and resisted the Patriots' demand to declare their opposition to the Crown.

» Many Loyalists realized that independence was bound to come eventually, but they were fearful that revolution might lead to anarchy, tyranny, or mob rule. In contrast, the prevailing attitude among Patriots, who made systematic efforts to use mob violence in a controlled manner, was a desire to seize the initiative.

» Loyalists were pessimists who lacked the confidence in the future that the Patriots displayed.

As you read Labaree's list, you can almost feel the tension between the Loyalists—who had it pretty good under the British and wanted to preserve things—and the Patriots, who believed in their guts that more people could prosper if they were free of England.

How is that similar to today?

Well, power and wealth have been concentrating in the hands and wallets of fewer and fewer Americans, what many now call the "One Percent." And for many Americans, the dreamy parts of the American Dream seem farther away. Those who are oldest and most established seem to have it pretty good. Those who are youngest and least established see their chances slimming.

It took the American Revolution to crack the cask of power, and spill the benefits of liberty to more people.

*It's a matter of taking the side of the weak against the
strong, something the best people have always done.*

Harriet Beecher Stowe

America's Second Winter:

The Civil War & Reconstruction, 1860-1877

It's ironic that America was founded on the idea that "all men are born free" . . . and then the nation went on to enslave millions of Africans. Indeed, the seeds of our second winter were already scattered during our first; almost immediately after America declared itself free from Britain, the states were asking, "Are slaves entitled to the same rights of the new Constitution as Europeans?"

It took until President Lincoln's election in 1860 for the spark to ignite, and for America's second winter to begin.

You see, in the 74 years between American independence and the Civil War, two Americas emerged: the North and the South. The South's economy grew out of agriculture: a plantation system powered largely by slavery. The North's economy was more diverse—family farms, industry, mining, and commerce. And the North had a lot of momentum on its side. The North was growing quickly.

So along came presidential candidate Abraham Lincoln in 1859, a guy from Illinois, a.k.a. the North. He was an attorney, not a plantation owner. And his party, the Republican Party, was sympathetic to the

North's key issues: higher tariffs (taxes), nationalism (over states' rights), and abolishing slavery.[8]

The North loved Lincoln. The South loathed him. Lincoln's name wasn't even on the ballot in 10 Southern states.

But Lincoln didn't need the South's votes to win the presidency. Due to its rapid growth, the North's share of the Electoral College was enough to elect Lincoln and send him to the White House.

Immediately after Lincoln's election, South Carolina, Mississippi, Florida, Alabama, Georgia, Louisiana, and Texas formed the Confederate States of America and declared secession. How's that for a first week as president?

Lincoln tried to placate the South and keep the United States together, but it couldn't be done. To say that the South was mad is like saying that Grover Norquist dislikes taxes.

The Civil War started shortly after Lincoln took office, pitting the Unionists (mostly from the North, who wanted the United States to remain together) against the Confederates (mostly from the South, who wanted to split off from the United States).

---

8   Yes, it's true: Lincoln's Republicans favored higher taxes and nationalism over statism. President Lincoln probably wouldn't recognize the Republicans of early 21st century America, proof that people (and parties) change.

The Civil War was long, and it was bloody. By the time it ended in 1865, it had claimed the lives of 620,000 soldiers and saw untold civilian casualties. Our country was torn apart. But the war's end was not the end of our second winter. In winters, bad news and hardship pile on, and the country gets stuck in a funk.

That's what happened after the Civil War ended. A funk. America began Reconstruction, which was intended to rejoin the Confederacy to the Union and extend constitutional and legal status to blacks. But it was more like trying to sew one person's top half onto another person's bottom half. It was ugly and painful and disjointed. It caused deep suffering for people on both sides of the issue. Reconstruction had a few high points ... but mostly low points.

The most radical phase of Reconstruction occurred between 1866 and 1871, when three amendments were added to the Constitution:

(1) The Thirteenth Amendment abolished slavery and involuntary servitude.

(2) The Fourteenth Amendment overruled Dred Scott, declaring once and for all that blacks were and could become American citizens.

(3) The Fifteenth Amendment prohibited each government in the United States from denying a citizen the right to vote based on the individual's "race, color, or previous condition of servitude."

Remember, we said that one of the themes of winter is that it usually extends more rights to more people? You see that here; Reconstruction expanded legal rights and citizenship to blacks who'd served as slaves in America's first 80 years. But these legal gains were painfully won . . . and existed mostly on paper. For black Americans, this period was a triumph, but only for a split second. As W. E. B. Du Bois wrote in *Black Reconstruction in America* (1935): "The slave went free; stood for a brief moment in the sun; then moved back again toward slavery."

Of all of America's winters, the Civil War and Reconstruction period was our heaviest. The death toll of the Civil War was high, and the pain of Reconstruction was real for everyone:

» Blacks won their freedom constitutionally but in reality continued to face discrimination. They were reabsorbed into society mostly as second-class citizens.

» White Northerners who stood with Lincoln won the war and helped make important legal strides, but both accomplishments came at a dear price personally, professionally, and emotionally.

» White Southerners felt they suffered worst of all. The Civil War and Reconstruction stole their livelihoods, their rights, and their pride. They fought Reconstruction with every ounce of their energy.

What does the Civil War and Reconstruction period teach us? Building on the previous three lessons from the American Revolution:

{4}

Sometimes, winter brings gains in one area, but those gains don't become fully realized until much, much later. During the Civil War and Reconstruction, we passed three (three!) constitutional amendments, which expanded more rights and freedoms to blacks. But the country was so tired, so socially fractured, and attitudes toward slavery in America were so volatile that it would take nearly one hundred years— until the 1960s and the Youth Movement—for society's feelings and behaviors toward African Americans to shift and catch up to those policies.

Now I know some of you are wondering, "If Reconstruction was so anticlimactic, how did America emerge from winter to spring?"

Here's how I see it. And it's an important, additional insight:

{5}

America emerged from winter to spring because our economic prosperity eventually overshadowed our social unrest.

Remember, before President Lincoln was elected, the North was already bursting economically. This continued after the Civil War as new railroads were built and the steam engine came chugging along. Factories were opening. Unions were forming. America was entering the Gilded Age, a period of broad economic expansion when the United States surpassed Britain as the global leader in manufacturing and many new inventions and discoveries were made.

Mark Twain and Charles Dudley Warner's 1873 novel, *The Gilded Age: A Tale of Today,* summarized and satirized this odd juxtaposition: in America after Reconstruction, a layer of gold covered our country's deep differences in values.

The Great Depression in the United States, far from being a sign of the inherent instability of the private enterprise system, is a testament to how much harm can be done by mistakes on the part of a few men when they wield vast power over the monetary system of a country.

Milton Friedman, *Capitalism and Freedom,* 1962

America's Third Winter:
The Great Depression, 1929-1941

Sometimes, things get worse over the weekend.

On Thursday, October 24, 1929, prices on the New York Stock Exchange fell abruptly. A group of leading bankers freaked out and called a private meeting to stop the market's losses. They pooled their resources and bought up shares of U.S. Steel and other large companies' stocks.

It worked.

For a day.

On Saturday and Sunday while the stock market was closed, Americans devoured newspaper stories about the market's fall. By Monday, everyday investors pulled out of the stock market in droves, driving the market even lower. The Dow lost 13 percent of its value on Monday, and another 12 percent on Tuesday. All told, the stock market lost $30 billion in two days. "Black Monday" and "Black Tuesday" led to a chain reaction of events that resulted in the Great Depression.

Some Americans have contrasted our latest Great Recession with the Great Depression. In reality, the Depression was worse. During that period:

» Unemployment held steady between 11 percent and its peak, 25 percent.

» Americans who were lucky enough to have jobs saw their wages fall by 42 percent.

» Unsophisticated farming methods and a terrible drought caused the American Plains "Dust Bowl" in the early 1930s, which left more than 500,000 Americans homeless.

» By 1940, 2.5 million people had moved out of the Plains states. The Dust Bowl exodus (mostly from Kansas and Oklahoma) was the largest migration in American history within such a short length of time.[9]

» More than 250,000 American teenagers left their homes and hopped onto empty railroad cars, crisscrossing the country in an attempt to find work.[10]

The Great Depression was also significantly different than our previous two winters. Our first and second winters, the American Revolution and the Civil War, required bloody sacrifice. They pitted man against man, brother against brother. They were wars of ideals: that all men are born free (American Revolution), and that America must hold together

---

9   "Dust Bowl," *Wikipedia*, http://en.wikipedia.org/wiki/Dust_Bowl, accessed November 2, 2012.

10   Errol Lincoln Uys, introduction to *Riding the Rails: Teenagers on the Move During the Great Depression* (New York: Routledge, 2003), i.

as a single union, with the same laws and freedoms applied to all (Civil War).

The Great Depression was different. It wasn't a war between men or a war for ideals. It was a struggle to regain financial footing after two invisible forces—the stock market's crash and the Dust Bowl—eviscerated financial gain and stability in a few punishing strokes.

Although the enemy was different, the challenge was similar. The Great Depression asked Americans deep, fundamental questions: What do we believe in? For what and for whom will our laws stand?

Under President Roosevelt's leadership, America responded that we stood for economic protection against hardship. We stood *for* fair markets where investors could see what they were buying. We stood *against* reckless banking and run-ups in housing prices and for protecting the unemployed, the elderly, the poor, and America's farmers.

President Roosevelt designed a package of initiatives to restore confidence. He called them the "Three Rs": Relief for the unemployed and poor, recovery of the economy to 1929 levels, and reform of the financial system to prevent a repeat depression.

Many programs that sprang out of the Three Rs are still in service today: Social Security, the Federal Deposit Insurance Corporation

(FDIC), the Federal Crop Insurance Corporation (FCIC), the Federal Housing Administration (FHA), and the Securities and Exchange Commission (SEC).

What can we learn from the Great Depression?

{6}

Winter is a period when bad news piles on. This causes a rational and emotional funk. Our heads and our hearts get heavy. The Great Depression would've been bad enough if the stock market's crash was the only thing we had going against us. But when you add a drought, and half a million people leaving their homes, and a quarter of a million kids starting to ride the rails like hobos, it starts to feel like Armageddon.

In our current winter, we've had the piling on of bad news, too. You know the rap sheet: financial system collapse, high unemployment, home foreclosures, Wall Street bankers walking off with larger paychecks than ever, drought across the American Midwest.

{7}

America finally shook off the Great Depression—when we entered World War II. We were hesitant to enter the war, but once we did: Whammo! The economy snapped to life. Men went to war. Women went to work. The whole country unified and mobilized to Win This Thing.

After the war, with our infrastructure unblemished and our allies badly wounded, ours was the only developed economy still standing. And it took off at a full sprint.

The moral of the story: sometimes it takes a good old-fashioned national crisis to jolt our country out of its funk and focus on a larger, unifying issue.

{8}

A final lesson is the role that a leader can play during a crisis, to fortify our confidence and guide us forward. President Roosevelt served as our Narrator in Chief during the Great Depression. His fireside chats, which always opened with "Dear friends," used modern technology (radio) to open the lines of communication with all Americans. He spoke in plain language to explain the crises and his approach to them. His speech was sure-footed. He was sometimes comforting or inspiring. ("The only thing we have to fear is fear itself.") And Americans responded.

Following his chats, citizens flooded the White House with letters, which Roosevelt read and sometimes used to persuade Congress to adopt certain policies. President Roosevelt's commitment to talk regularly with Americans—he gave thirty fireside chats over several years—allowed him to lead, reassure, and mobilize the nation during a difficult time.

For years, we've grown dependant on American consumers as the world's spenders of last resort. They've kept Europe out of recession, allowed China to industrialise, and prevented global deflation. But at the same time, they've not been looking after their own futures.

British economist and journalist Evan Davis, 2009

America's Fourth Winter:
The Great Recession, 2001-2020 (est.)

That brings us to today, America's fourth winter.

It's tempting to think that our current winter started in September 2008 when Lehmann Brothers collapsed. It didn't. Our current winter began like all winters do—with a spark—a single event that sets off a chain reaction of "ick" that puts us in a funk. You can think of that spark as the first domino to fall, knocking down others as it goes.

The spark could be a piece of paper, like the Declaration of Independence. Or a president's election, like Lincoln's.

Our spark was 9/11, a well-orchestrated terrorist attack that put four planes on a crash course with high-profile American buildings.

But 9/11 was just the first domino to fall. By 2002, America's longest-running bear market came to a halt. The second domino.

To make up for its slowdown, Wall Street invented new tools to make money, what many now know as credit default swaps and over-leveraged assets. The Street created a long line of dominoes, which was fine, as long as they all kept standing. But as we know, they didn't.

The Levin-Coburn Report summarized the main causes of the financial crisis. You can see a list of all the dominoes that dutifully stood, and then fell one on top of another:

> The crisis was not a natural disaster, but the result of high risk, complex financial products; undisclosed conflicts of interest; and the failure of regulators, the credit rating agencies, and the market itself to rein in the excesses of Wall Street.[11]

The banks were eventually bailed out, but in their wake hundreds more dominoes have fallen: cities and pension funds have gone bankrupt; housing foreclosures and unemployment have created a rootless, anxious class; and the next bubble could be (dealer's choice): student loan debt, commercial real estate, or the global reinsurance market. Oh yeah, and China's economy has nearly flattened, which will have its own set of domino-like consequences.

America is not technically in a depression, according to economists, but many of us *feel* depressed. We wonder, like our forebears who limped through previous American winters, "When will things get back to 'normal?'"

---

11   Carl Levin, Tom Coburn, and the United States Senate Permanent Subcommittee on Investigations, *Wall Street and the Financial Crisis: Anatomy and a Financial Collapse* (April 13, 2011): 1–11, www.hsgac.senate.gov//imo/media/doc/Financial_Crisis/FinancialCrisisReport.pdf (accessed November 3, 2012).

My friends, there is no getting back to normal in the near term. What we've just lived through is a great upset. An upheaval. A natural period in an all-American lineup of seasons. Best-selling business author Jim Collins believes America is now entering "an extended period of uncertainty and disruption that might well characterize the rest of our lives."[12]

And what makes this period insidious compared to previous winters is that a lot of the fallout is *invisible*. We don't see bread lines, because now we have food stamps. We don't see our neighbors' financial angst; we just notice their house for sale. We don't know the emotional toll that three, four, five years of unemployment has taken on our family members. We don't see our fellow Americans suffer, but we can *feel* them suffer. We sense it, the piling on of real hardship and emotional stress.

Yes, things will get better. Eventually. But for many years to come, we'll be more careful with our spending. We'll learn to make do. We'll save more. We won't rely on anyone for a handout, and we'll read the fine print—in the credit card offers and the loan documents. We'll figure it out, with the help of our relatives. And our neighbors. And our friends.

And while we sort through the very personal and private economic wreckage of the past several years, America is also trying to sort itself

---

12   Geoff Colvin, "Jim Collins: In His Own Words," *Fortune*, September 30, 2011, http://management.fortune.cnn.com/2011/09/30/jim-collins-interview/   (accessed October 25, 2011).

out. Just like in previous winters, we're asking big questions about what it means to be an American, and what we need to do to get our mojo back.

Eight Lessons from Past Winters

All of our previous winters eventually ended, and ours will too.

When?

Good question. If history is our guide, it will take an average of 19.67 years, or through about 2020.

Winter	No. of Years	Spring Came With...
American Revolution	20	Treaty of Paris, which formalized U.S. independence from Britain
Civil War & Reconstruction	17	Economic boom and the "Gilded Age"
Great Depression	22	Government spending to enter World War II
Great Recession	??	??

What will finally help us turn the page from winter to spring?

It won't be sudden, or a single, spectacular event. We came out of our last two winters because of government investments—in the railroads after the Civil War, and in armaments for our entry into World War II. Spring unfolded gradually, and quietly.

Until then, here are the big lessons from our previous winters:

{1}

In hindsight, winters always seem obvious. The cause of a current winter is often visible years before winter actually arrives.

{2}

Winter causes America to question itself.

{3}

In winter, established elders will often fight to keep things the same, because the established systems work well for them.

Others, including youth or those who are progress-minded, fight to change things, because they believe that things should be better for more people, not just a single, established class.

{4}

Winters may bring gains in an area that aren't fully realized until much later.

During Reconstruction, three amendments were added
to the Constitution, but they weren't legally enforced
or socially embraced until 80 years later.

{5}

Winters may be "social," like the Civil War and
Reconstruction, or "economic," like the Great Depression.

{6}

During winter, bad news often piles on, like
dominoes falling over onto each other.

{7}

Sometimes it takes a national crisis, like
World War II, to jolt us out of winter.

{8}

Leaders play an important role during winter, to help
Americans understand the crisis, and our way forward.

Now that we've taken a walk through history to recall the lessons of previous winters, it's time to get to work, to sort out what's happening in this, our current winter. We've got some big work ahead of us, you and I, so let's get to it.

If we observed first and designed second,

we wouldn't need most of the things we build.

Ben Hamilton-Baillie

PART TWO: FIRST WHO; THEN WHAT

I'd like to talk about sidewalks. I realize this seems a bit off-topic, what with our focus on America's future and all, but as one of my favorite science teachers used to say, "If you stay with me, I promise we'll get to the point."

When I was studying at Drake University in the early 90s, I had a lot of classes in Meredith Hall. Meredith was a cool building. It was designed by starchitect Mies van der Rohe and is considered architecturally significant because rather than burying steel I-beams inside the building, Mies van der Rohe exposed them in the building's facade.

However ...

To get to Meredith, we didn't follow the pretty, winding sidewalks. We cut through Helmick Commons. We traipsed over manicured lawns. And on its east side, we cut through hedgerows.

I remember walking those paths mentally muttering, "Why are the beautiful sidewalks built *over there*, when everyone walks *over here*?" Why would Drake commission a world-famous architect and invest in so much glass and slate without ensuring that the final design and all of its arterial sidewalks worked in harmony with the building and the traffic patterns?

If Mies (or anyone) had simply planted himself in a lawn chair on the building's site and watched the traffic flow around campus, he could've anticipated how Meredith was going to fit within Drake's context. Instead, the design team made a critical mistake: they focused on *what* Mies was building and ignored *who* it was for and *how* it would be used.

This happens all the time.

We two-leggeds are constantly doing dumb things like building ornate sidewalks that no one uses because we aren't good analysts of our own behavior. Dutch psychologist Ap Dijksterhuis calls this inability to accurately predict what will be useful, or make us truly happy, a "weighting mistake," a classic decision-making error in which we lose sight of important variables, like our own happiness. Jonah Lehrer[13] wrote about this in his "Frontal Cortex" blog on March 30, 2010:

> Consider two housing options: a three bedroom apartment that is located in the middle of a city, with a ten minute commute time, or a five bedroom McMansion on the urban outskirts, with a forty-five minute commute.

> "People will think about this trade-off for a long time," Dijksterhuis says. "And most of them will eventually choose the large house. After all, a third bathroom or extra bedroom is very important for

---

13   Mr. Lehrer is a now-deposed science writer. An independent study found that he has plagiarized and recycled much of his work: www.slate.com/articles/health_and_science/science/2012/08/jonah_lehrer_plagiarism_in_wired_com_an_investigation_into_plagiarism_quotes_and_factual_inaccuracies_single.html. That said, I use this citation because it includes direct quotes from Mr. Dijksterhuis, which have not been found to be false, plagiarized, or misleading.

when grandma and grandpa come over for Christmas, whereas driving two hours each day is really not that bad." What's interesting, Dijksterhuis says, is that the more time people spend deliberating, the more important that extra space becomes. They'll imagine all sorts of scenarios (a big birthday party, Thanksgiving dinner, another child) that will turn the suburban house into an absolute necessity. The pain of a lengthy commute, meanwhile, will seem less and less significant, at least when compared to the allure of an extra bathroom. But, as Dijksterhuis points out, that reasoning process is exactly backwards: "The additional bathroom is a completely superfluous asset for at least 362 or 363 days each year, whereas a long commute does become a burden after a while."

By over-focusing on *what* we're building, buying, or creating, we under-focus on *who* it's for, and *how* it will be used.

So let's tie all this back to our thesis.

If America is going to regenerate—to work better for more people— we have to put people back in the center of our thinking. We have to deeply consider *whom* we're regenerating for, and *how* their lives will be.

It takes discipline to think this way. Following are some of my favorite examples of how people get plowed under as systems develop over time:

Cities are for *people* (not cars)

Schools are for *learners* (not unions)

Homes are for *families* (not developers)

Products are for *customers* (not the engineers who conceive them)

Hospitals are for *patients* (not health insurance companies)

Government is of, by, and for the *people* (not politicians or PACs)

I'm not writing this to be political (although I'm sure my list raises some hackles). I'm being practical. Proper design puts people first. And if America is going to regenerate in a way we can all be proud of, you and I need to do what that architect should've done: plunk our lawn chairs down in the Commons and see who will populate America's future and how they'll be living, before we start digging holes.

So let's do that. Let's take a bird's-eye view of who Americans are and how they'll be living.

Imagine it's 10 years from today.

How old are you?

What life stage are you in?

Are you single? Married? Divorced? Widowed?

Where are you in your career? Just starting out? Hitting your stride? Coasting toward retirement? Working or volunteering post-retirement?

What about your education? Are you in school full-time? Back for a degree on evenings and weekends? Auditing courses to "stay fresh"? Or getting your PhD in the school of hard knocks?

Are you living alone, with someone, or in a multigenerational household that includes aging parents or kids who've boomeranged back home?

Do you have a picture in mind, a picture of yourself in ten years?

Good.

Now let's zoom out and look at the six generations that will pepper America in 2020 and 2030:

Generations in America, 2013, 2020, 2030

American Generation	Birth Years	Age in 2013 (mid-winter)	Age in 2020 (spring, est.)	Age in 2030 (mid-spring)
G.I.	1901-1924	89-112	96-119	Deceased
Silent	1925-1945	68-88	75-95	85-105
Baby Boomer	1946-1964	49-67	56-74	66-85
Gen Xer	1965-1980	33-48	40-55	50-65
Millennial	1981-2001	12-32	19-39	29-49
iGeneration	2002-2020 (est.)	0-11	0-18	10-28

What will life be like for America's generations as we turn move from winter into spring? A few speculations:

By 2020, half of all Boomers will be eligible for retirement.[14] But don't expect them to buy Cadillacs and drive south. They're reinventing retirement. They're living longer and more healthfully than their parents and grandparents did, and although Boomers may be sheepish to admit this, many didn't save enough for retirement.[15] They need to stay in the workforce longer. And they *want* to.

Boomers daydream about their "encore careers." Working with a nonprofit, maybe. Or starting that quaint coffee shop or boutique on a quiet street where life feels less frantic. Wherever and whenever they "retire," Boomers want to make a difference, and they will use their legacy years to channel their wisdom and experience to that end. They will be more connected to their children and grandchildren than their parents were, and although their bodies will get older, their hearts will stay "forever young."

Of course, America needs Boomers to remember their youth—what they believed in, marched for, sat-in for, and spoke out for. Boomers must find the strength and courage to channel the gifts of elderhood—wisdom, maturity, a sense of mortality—to ensure that their grandchildren and

---

14   Not that they will retire; their successors, Gen Xers, refer to Boomers at work as the "gray ceiling."

15   Blaire Briody, "5 Reasons Boomers Will Go Bust," *Fiscal Times*, July 23, 2012, http://money.msn.com/baby-boomers/5-reasons-boomers-will-go-bust-fiscaltimes.aspx (accessed November 24, 2012).

great-grandchildren inherit the world Boomers dreamed about when they were young, a world that is more equal and more just.

By 2030, Gen Xers will lead most American organizations: public, profit, nonprofit, and civic. Compared to Boomers, Xers are less idealistic and more practical. Where Boomers set out to change the world, Xers focus on fixing it. Xers are dubious of silver bullets or grand compromises. In the words of Xer Cameron Sinclair, cofounder of Architecture for Humanity and winner of the TED Prize, "Utopia is dead. What [we] need is not one solution but a hundred million solutions."[16] Xers will focus with laser-like precision on eliminating waste, middlemen, and bureaucracy wherever they exist. Where there is a margin, they will squeeze it.

Xers will lead America across the rickety bridge between the way things used to work and the way they will work. Xers' job is to help America cross the bridge, and then burn it behind them.

At work, Xers will labor side by side with people from all levels within organizations. Xers will be as interested in the opinions of junior staffers as they are in those of so-called experts. Xers' teams will have a diversity of worldviews, sexual orientations, ethnic backgrounds, family structures, and political-mindedness. Political correctness—not saying something for fear it will offend someone—will be replaced

---

16   Jeff Gordinier, *X Saves the World: How Gen X Got the Shaft But Can Still Keep Everything from Sucking* (New York: Hudson Books, 2008), 157.

with open and respectful dialogue where differences are not only talked about, they are backed with facts to drive necessary change.

At home, Xers are late bloomers. They married later, sometimes in their mid- to late 20s or early 30s, and many of those were starter marriages. By 2030, many of them, even those in their 50s, will still have kids in elementary school. Their families will be more diverse than ever; they've married across races and within genders. Because they started their families later, many have adopted children from around the world, especially Korea, Guatemala, Russia, and China.

At home and at work, Xers' reputation will be practical and tough. Xers won't earn the kind of money they thought they could, but they're learning to live on less. They don't have the executive jobs they hoped to have, but they're finding a way to make a difference anyway. And they may not be able to give their kids everything they'd like to, but Xers have raised their kids to be practical and resourceful. Like them.

By 2030, the large Millennial population will be absorbed into the workforce. Yes, they got a slow start, landing in the job market around the time of the Great Recession. To cope, many went back to school for additional degrees or limped from job to job while crashing at their parents' places. They didn't mind; unlike Gen Xers, Millennials never felt like losers about moving home after college. Besides, Millennials are friends with their parents. The generation gap that Boomers blew open has been closed by Millennials, who share their parents' and grandparents' values at home and at work.

At work, Millennials will earn reputations as confident, trusting, and teachable. They'll prove themselves more collaborative than Xers, but less innovative. Millennials will perform exceptionally well when managed with clear instructions and a sense of purpose. Because they entered the workforce during turbulence, they're gun-shy about taking risk; Millennials prefer job security over a chance at high-stakes rewards.

Socially and politically, Millennials will be active. They were important swing votes in President Obama's elections, and their presence and views continue to shape politics as they become the new demographic bulge. Millennials' consumer activism will drive companies to be more clear and transparent about their environmental impacts and corporate social responsibility.

Millennials will have a hard time understanding why so many older Americans, even their own grandparents, are still hung up on issues like immigration and gay marriage when there are other, more important problems in the world—like the fact that the planet is getting hotter or that they may never pay off their student debt.

If you're a member of the iGeneration, your entire K–16 education experience was more diverse than that of your parents, grandparents, or great-grandparents. One in four of your classmates is Latino; half are white, and 2 out of 10 are black. You know that today's families come in all kinds of configurations: one parent, two parents, three or four parents; Mom and Dad, two moms, two dads. It's hard for your parents to keep it all straight, but you don't mind. Your parents may struggle with your classmates' "unusual" names, but it's easy for you. This is the way it's always been.

What's not easy is figuring out what your future holds. Does college make sense? It seems so expensive, and the job market seems bleak. You understand why youth in Tunisia and Syria and Egypt revolted in 2011. Like you, they feel that their futures may not be as bright as they'd hoped. Your parents try to shield you from this, but what it really feels like is suffocation. You have important ideas on how to change the world, and your creative perspective is needed, but often missing, from the conversation.

****

These are the broad generational outlines of who America will be in 2020, 2030, and beyond. How do these descriptions resonate with you? Your family? Your neighborhood? Can you see where America is headed?

Two major demographic headwinds will sweep across America as we regenerate from winter to spring: (1) America is becoming an older country; (2) We're becoming far more diverse. I call these two trends the graying and browning of America. What happens when a mostly white older population and a more diverse younger population live together in the same country? We're about to find out. Here's the short version: the generation gap that emerged between Boomers and their elders will be replaced by a cultural generation gap[17] between younger, multicultural Americans and older, more homogenous Americans.

For the left-brained among us, some stats may be in order. And because my mom raised me right, let's start with our elders:

The US census and population projections show that:

» From now to 2050, Americans over 65 as a group will grow faster than those aged 0–19 or 20–64. (Kinda explains all those Viagra commercials, doesn't it?)

» By 2025, the 65-plus age cohort will be nearly 18 percent of the population, compared to 12.4 percent of the population in 2000.

America is getting older for two reasons.

First, the enormous Baby Boom generation is aging. The year 2011 was a watershed, when the oldest Boomer turned 65. Now, wrap your head around this: in 2011, an average of 7,000 Boomers turned 65 each day.

---

17   I first heard William Frey of the Brookings Institution use this expression, and it perfectly summarizes the near-term impact America is likely to feel from our graying and browning populations.

That's 2.5 million new 65-year-olds every year, the equivalent of adding a retiree Rome or a senior San Diego to America's population each year.

The second reason our older population is growing is because Americans are living longer. One hundred years ago, your great-great-grandpap was dead by 56. But if you're breathing today (and I assume you are, because you're reading this), you're likely to live 'til 80. (Congratulations.) And if you're born today—into a middle-class family anywhere in the world—you will almost certainly reach your 100th birthday. (Buckle up, newborns.) I heard a futurist say recently that it's very likely that today's kids will reach their 120th or 150th birthdays. Holy crap.

Now let's turn the page and talk about the other main trend, the browning of America.

By 2020, America will be more multicultural and less white. The statistics point to a significant demographic change that will sweep through every state.

Here's what we know about the browning of America:

» Between 2000 and 2010, 98 percent of all population growth in America's largest cities came from nonwhites, and 83 percent of the country's population growth came from nonwhites.

» Forty percent of infants in more than half of all states are minorities. The white share of infants is declining in all states except the District of Columbia.

» Latinos are quickly becoming the United States' largest minority. By 2050, one in three Americans will be of Latino origin, and blacks will remain consistent at about 13 percent of the population.

» Blacks represent the largest minority in 17 states—all in the South plus Michigan, Missouri, Ohio, and Pennsylvania.

Figure 2: Percentage of Infants Under 1 Who are Non-White, Source: Brookings Institution

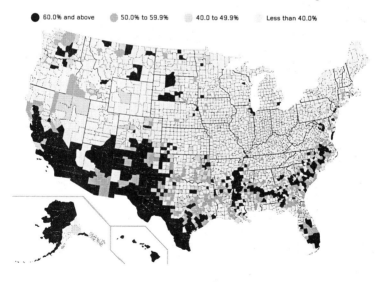

● 60.0% and above   ◕ 50.0% to 59.9%   ◔ 40.0 to 49.9%   Less than 40.0%

» In 2011, one in every two babies born in America was nonwhite (see Figure 2).

To understand the generational shift that is taking place, consider that minorities make up 15 percent of those aged 85 and older and nearly half of the under-5 age group.

Statistics also suggest that New America—at least the workforce—will be more female and less male.[18] By 2020, American women will be midway through a multiyear record-breaking streak: their salaries will surpass their husbands'; they will hold more seats in Congress than ever before; and the percentage of women who are CEOs, Fortune 500 board members, and nonprofit and education leaders will be at record highs.

Looking back, the 2012 all-white-male, non-Tweeting Republican presidential ticket will go down as the last of its kind, a final homage to legacy America.

New America will change the map, and with it America's sensibilities. New America will demand fairer taxes and a contemporary immigration system. New America will fight for economic mobility and social justice. New America will be less Republican, less Democratic, and more independent, self-directed.

New Americans will color our country differently in the years to come. And some Americans will have a hard time dealing with it. But research

---

18   Did you know there are five million more women in America than there are men?

shows that although greater diversity is harder for communities in the short term, it's better in the long term.

Throw any mix of random people together, and you're sure to get some friction. Need proof? Think about Thanksgiving. Or how long it took you to warm up to your in-laws. Overcoming differences takes time.

But in time, we do meld and blend and discover each others' humanity— and our combined strength. That's when diversity's true potential emerges.

William Frey, a senior fellow at the Metropolitan Policy Program of the Brookings Institution (himself an older white guy), has looked these diversity trends squarely in the face and assures us that America's future diversity is our strength:

> Older Americans fear cuts to Medicare and Social Security, but they need to understand the long-term benefits for the country and for them, that will come from providing younger Americans the wherewithal for good education, housing support, and health care. Our young, diverse population will be the backbone of our labor force and will provide future business and government leadership, in a new American demographic era.[19]

---

19   William H. Frey, "America Reaches Its Demographic Tipping Point," www.brookings.edu/blogs/up-front/posts/2011/08/26-census-race-frey, accessed November 4, 2012.

These two demographic gusts—the browning and graying of our country—will make America older and more culturally diverse . . . in 2020 and for years to come. These are not speculations or guesses; they are facts. What we do with those facts is up to us.

Now let's add one final layer to our perspective of America in the future: how technology will impact us. Powered by smaller, more powerful tools and bigger data sets, what once seemed impossible will be gorgeously, magically commonplace:

» Google's self-driving car may not be available on the mass market yet, but bridges and streets will monitor themselves for precipitation, ice, and traffic and self-adjust their surfaces and stoplights for safer, smoother transit.

» See something you like on Amazon? Print it off at home with a 3D printer.[20]

» Does your child have a fever? Have her swallow a small digital pill, affix a disposable patch to her arm, and turn on your smartphone. You (or your doctor) can see what's up.

---

20   Peter Diamandis and Teven Kotler, *Abundance: The Future Is Better than You Think* (New York: Free Press, 2012), 70–79.

» Have you been to visit three doctors and still don't know why you're sick? IBM's Watson will gather your test results and diagnose you within minutes. Watson can ingest more data in a day than a mortal doctor can in a lifetime and "can read all the world's medical journals in less time than it takes a physician to drink a cup of coffee."[21]

» Our first generation of open-source college graduates will tout degrees of their own design, learning from top professors at MIT, Stanford, Harvard, and others.

» Thanks to open data, residents will know which local schools have the best ratings, the best route to take to work based on real-time traffic, which restaurants have the best (and worst) health rankings, and which landlords are the most responsible . . . all available on their smartphones.

America in 2020 will look *and* act much differently than it did at the start of winter, in 2001, before Facebook and the iPhone, before Obama and Palin, before Twitter and the Arab Spring, before the Tea Party and Occupy Wall Street. A lot can happen in a couple of decades.

---

21   Jon Gertner, "Calling Doctor Watson," *Fast Company* (November 2012), 126.

An unwillingness to acknowledge or address problems is a classic way to avoid the future—it is also a classic form of foolishness, the antithesis of wisdom.

Tom Lombardo, Center for Future Consciousness

PART THREE: SIX QUESTIONS FOR REGENERATION

You know Dr. Phil, the bald, drawling psychologist whom Oprah made famous in the late 1990s with "Tuesdays with Doctor Phil"? I always get a chuckle out of watching his show. He has a certain "aw, shucks" veneer that draws you in. On air, he listens to guests describe their issues: their morbidly overweight nine-year-old, their sexless marriage, their mountain of debt.

Dr. Phil sits and patiently listens. Eventually, he starts asking more and more pointed questions about the guest's habits or behaviors. You know, the kind of stuff that causes your kid to be a couch potato, or your marriage to dry up, or your credit cards to max.

And as soon as they fess up about their behavior, Dr. Phil lowers the hammer and asks, "How's that workin' for ya?"

The message is always the same: you get the results you deserve.

I imagine if Dr. Phil were sitting here reading this book with us, he'd start in with his questions . . . about how we feel about the current winter and what we think caused it. And at a certain point, he'd have us sort of backed into a corner, making connections between our behavior and the pickle we've gotten ourselves into. Maybe we haven't voted as often as we could've. Maybe we haven't saved enough for retirement, or we bought too much crap on credit. Or maybe we're wasting too much time liking our friends' posts on Facebook and we're just not as up on issues as we could be.

And right before a commercial break, Dr. Phil would look us square in the eye and ask, "How's that workin' for ya?"

The truth is, this period of winter isn't just for the feds in Washington, DC. Winter requires greater responsibility and reflection from all of us. I know you may be thinking: "These issues are too complex for me to understand," or "Who am I to address this stuff? I don't have a degree in economics!" or "This mess is for someone else to fix. I just want to live my life."

I understand your misgivings. I have them, too. But who are we *not* to look deeply at our country? Who—if not us—will push, pull, nudge, and cannonball our nation through winter and into spring? Look around, our leaders are failing us! We can't wait for someone else to do it for us. We gotta get in there and do some heavy lifting.

Our willingness to face our challenges, to look these issues squarely in the eye, to discuss them—even with people with whom we disagree— are the small but heroic acts that will help scatter the seeds of spring.

So let's get on with it, shall we? The following essays are organized as the Big Questions I believe America must address, to make sure that come spring, America works better for more people.

I'm a senior myself, so I can talk about this.

I think a country that gives priority to its old over its young

doesn't have much of a future.

Isabel V. Sawhill

Question 1: How Will We Balance the Needs of Our Children with the Needs of Our Elders?

Intergenerational equity is one of America's fundamental propositions. To paraphrase, intergenerational equity calls on all of us—youth, adult, and elderly—to be our brother's keeper, to take care of our own needs without impacting another generation's ability to do the same.

At home, intergenerational equity is the reason we set up 529 education savings plans for our kids and try to keep enough back so we can leave an inheritance. We want our next generation to have it better than we did, and we are willing to sacrifice a little bit today so that they can have an easier go of it tomorrow.

The opposite of intergenerational equity is something like this: parents who buy a brand-new, enormous oceanfront house and finance it with a jumbo loan that comes due—all the principal and interest—after they die. And it's payable only by their kids; it can't be written off posthumously. It saddles children with debt they didn't choose and an asset they can't afford. It's simply unfair.

This jumbo loan example, however, is pretty close to the situation America has brewed up for itself. Our seniors are expecting entitlements (Social Security, Medicare, and Medicaid) to which they have a right. But their kids and grandkids simply cannot afford them.

The Congressional Budget Office predicts that by 2025, if we do nothing to change the level of entitlements seniors receive, 100 percent of the federal budget will be required to meet those commitments. We won't have any money left for education, the National Park Service, the Food and Drug Administration, our embassies, the army, navy, air force, marine corps, coast guard, federal courts, or prisons.

What's more, there's a vast discrepancy between what we spend on our elders versus our kids. Right now, the spending ratio on elders to children is 2.4 to 1. If you include the federal budget, the ratio is 7 to 1.[22]

There are several reasons the United States has gotten so intergenerationally misaligned, and I list them here so we can all get on the same page:

» *Baby Boomer bulge.* As this huge generation ages, they will drop out of the labor force and cross over from paying into the system to receiving payouts. And there are fewer working-age adults behind the Boomers who can pay into the system to support their retirement.

---

22   Julia Burrows, "Spending on Children and the Elderly," Brookings Institution (November 2009), 1, www.brookings.edu/research/reports/2009/11/05-spending-children-isaacs, accessed January 8, 2012.

» *Americans are living longer.* The Social Security age of 65 was set in 1935. Today we are living 26 percent longer, but Social Security's eligibility age has increased only 3 percent, to 67 years old.[23]

» *Extending life is expensive.* Few of us really want to die, and thanks to medical advances, we can put it off for a long time. But it's expensive to do so. Harvard economist David M. Cutler researched health care costs and outcomes from 1960 to 2000. He found that it took $46,870 to add one year to the life expectancy of a 65-year-old in the 1970s. By the 1990s, adjusted for inflation, it cost $145,000.[24]

» *Deficits are funded by foreigners.* The deficits created by Medicare and Medicaid are currently funded by foreigners at relatively low rates of interest. But as early as this year (2013), interest rates may begin to increase, and eventually, those debts will be called. Our children will be asked to pay.

To be blunt: many years ago America wrote its seniors a check that it now can't afford to cash. Yes, seniors are entitled to Social Security, Medicare, and Medicaid benefits under law, but it doesn't make the payout less ominous.

---

23   Mary Meeker, "USA Inc: Red, White, and Very Blue," *Bloomberg Businessweek*, February 24, 2011, www.businessweek.com/printer/articles/54850-usa-inc-dot-red-white-and-very-blue, accessed November 23, 2012 (hereafter referred to as USA).

24   David Brown, "We All Want Longer, Healthier Lives. But It's Going to Cost Us," *Washington Post* (January 11, 2009), www.washingtonpost.com/wp-dyn/content/article/2009/01/09/AR2009010902296_pf.html, accessed November 23, 2012.

Meanwhile, how are our kids doing? They don't have a powerful PAC like AARP to lobby for them . . . and it shows.

» The United States ranks 20th out of the 21 richest countries in overall child well-being. Specifically, the United States ranks 12th in education; 17th in material well-being; and 20th in health and safety, family/peer relationships, and behaviors and risks.[25]

» On the Programme for International Student Assessment (PISA) of 15-year-olds, the United States performs around the average in reading (rank 14th out of 34 developed countries) and science (17th) and below the average in mathematics (25th).[26] As Mary Meeker notes in her USA, *Inc.* report, "Any CEO will tell you that it's impossible to be best in class with a workforce that's outclassed."

» In 2006 the Urban Institute found that America invested $207 billion of the federal budget in children, mostly education and health care. That same year, the Bush tax cuts[27] equaled $233 billion.

America is on track to become a nation of well-cared-for older folks and underprepared young folks. Our priorities have gotten out of whack.

---

25   *Child Poverty in Perspective: An Overview of Child Well-Being in Rich Countries,* 2007, Innocenti Report Card 7, UNICEF Innocenti Research Centre (Florence, Italy, 2007), www.unicef-irc.org/publications/pdf/rc7_eng.pdf, accessed November 25, 2012.

26   OECD, *Lessons from PISA for the United States,* Strong Performers and Successful Reformers in Education, OECD Publishing, http://dx.doi.org/10.1787/9789264096660-en.

27   These tax cuts were for households with more than $200,000 in annual income.

Isabel Sawhill is one of America's foremost policy experts on this topic. In a speech titled "The Intergenerational Balancing Act: Where Children Fit in an Aging Society," she challenged her audience:

> Ask yourself if you were given $100,000 would you rather that it be invested in you when you were young or when you were old? Of course a lot might depend on your circumstances. No one would want to reduce the benefits going to an impoverished widow to give them to an affluent child. But that is not the trade-off we face. Instead, our social insurance programs provide benefits to all of the elderly—even Bill Gates. With the possible exception of public education, this is not true of the benefits we provide to children.

Most of us, even America's elders who are the recipients of entitlements, can see the need for course correction:

> As a member of the AARP generation I speak to my peers and we all come to the same conclusion: DO SOMETHING! At a time when so many of our fellow citizens are making sacrifices, we too should be able to do something. Yes, the benefits are wonderful. But those children and grandchildren we so love will pay the price. Is this an outcome we can live with? —Doris Fenig, Floral Park, NY

As someone who has reached the age of 80, I would hope that if there is any wisdom at all among my peer group, it will be to recognize that our duty is more to those coming after us than to ourselves. We have made it to old age, if AARP can bring about a sober dialogue between the young and us about how best to allocate resources fairly while saving Medicare, it would be common civic sense. —Daniel Callahand, president emeritus of the Hastings Center[28]

So what's America to do? Simply raising taxes is not enough. There is no feasible level of taxation that could cover entitlements' costs.

If raising taxes isn't the solution, what is? Sawhill again:

The solution, I would argue, is a new social contract between the young and the old. This revised intergenerational contract would invest more resources in the young, making them more productive, but it would then expect them to save more from this enhanced income to pay for their own and their parents' retirement. A bipartisan agreement to invest more in children now in return for a gradual phase-in of cost-saving reforms in entitlement programs is the most obvious way to accomplish this goal. These reforms could involve slowly raising the retirement age and indexing it

---

28   Both quotes are from "Sunday Dialogue: The Old, The Young, and Medicare," *New York Times*, July 3, 2011.

for longevity and asking more affluent seniors to pay for a larger share of their health care over time.

Social insurance was never meant to be the sole source of income in old age. It was meant to be one leg of a three-legged stool with the other two legs being private savings and employer pensions or 401K plans. Indeed, the basic notion behind any kind of insurance is that it should cover risks that people cannot predict. Yet everyone knows that they will someday be old and that their health care expenses will rise with age. They should therefore be expected to save for this eventuality. That way, our current social insurance programs could be tilted much more toward providing assistance to two groups among the elderly: those who experience a catastrophic or unexpected illness or disability and those who worked in lower-wage jobs for most of their lives and thus cannot afford to save enough to cover even the routine expenses of retirement.

The savings from asking the more affluent elderly to save more for their own retirement along with higher revenue could then be used to both reduce the deficit and invest in children—both of which would improve the rate of economic growth, increase the revenues needed to pay for current commitments, and produce a more prosperous and competitive nation for the future.[29]

I like Sawhill's recommendation because it steers us out of the intergenerational ditch and puts us back on a course toward intergenerational equity. It invests on the front end in our children and asks more of them down the road. It also asks seniors to do more for themselves, leaving the lion's share of elder entitlements to those who most need them.

On its surface, Sawhill's solution is rational. And responsible. But as we know, people aren't always rational. Or responsible.

I was giving a talk on intergenerational equity to a group of philanthropists in the Atlanta metro area. Philanthropists, I remind you, have so much money that they give lots of it away. For free. To charities.

After my talk, an older woman dressed neat as a pin in a beautiful Anne Klein suit and silk scarf approached me and said in that salty Southern drawl, "I enjoyed your talk. But don't even think about touching my Social Security. I paid in, and I expect to get my payout."

---

29   Isabel Sawhill, "The Intergenerational Balancing Act: Where Children Fit in an Aging Society," a paper given as a lecture on October 17, 2007, www.brookings.edu/~/media/research/files/speeches/2007/10/17useconomics%20sawhill/1017useconomics_sawhill, accessed October 8, 2012.

I can't know for sure, but based on the average net worth of her peers in the audience, I'd guess this woman didn't need her monthly Social Security check. She gave away more money in one year than she'd get in 20 years of Social Security. But she'd become attached to it. She saw it as hers. And she wasn't going to give it up without a fight.

In the absence of elders who are willing to sacrifice what they can so their kids and grandkids can have it as good as they did, I have one more wacky idea to help bring more intergenerational equity to our affairs: give kids the right to vote. Research shows that at age seven (plus or minus a year), most children have reached the age of reason.

Global organizations don't understand that the 21st century problem needs a 21st century solution. They work on top-down, government to government big programs and we're working on the slingshot, the little tool that David needs to take on Goliath.

Dean Kamen

Question 2: Top-Down? Bottom-Up? Open? Closed?

In Wisconsin, if you don't like how your mayor, school board member, congressperson, or governor is performing her or his duties, you can petition for a recall. This is what happened to Governor Scott Walker in 2011, after serving only one year in office.

Since I live in Madison, I had a front-row seat to the "Stand with Walker" versus "Recall Walker" battle. It was both thrilling and sad. Thrilling because voters got fired up about the democratic process: the right to petition, the right to free speech, the right to protest.

I believe deeply in democracy and love it when citizens exercise their rights.

But the recall process was also sad. It's time-consuming. It's expensive. It distracts electeds from governing. And it sure feels divisive.

Recalls are like bariatric surgery; they're intense, expensive ways to make up for previous decisions.

As you probably know, Governor Walker survived the recall election, but the lingering lessons about how the situation was handled will continue to be instructive for those of us bent on making America work better for more people.

At the center of this episode is a question for us: does America work better when it's top-down or bottom-up, when our systems have open information or closed?

There was a suspenseful moment in the recall process when those two operating systems clashed. You didn't hear much about it, but it was there. Let me take you inside the drama.

A bit of legalese: To force the recall, petitioners were required by Wisconsin's constitution to gather signatures from at least 540,208 eligible voters, 25 percent of the total 2010 voting populace, within 60 days. Time was of the essence.

Cleverly, a Walker supporter filed recall papers on November 4, 2011, 11 days before the Democratic Party of Wisconsin had planned to file its petition. Why would a supporter of the governor file recall papers against him? For two reasons: that action started the 60-day meter running before the Democrats were set to mobilize, and it allowed Republicans to start making contributions to Walker's campaign to fight the effort.

Yet by November 27, more than 300,000 recall signatures had reportedly been collected. And then mysteriously, the Democratic Party, which had been so boisterous at the recall's start, went silent.

It was eerie. Weeks went by without an update. Democrats wondered, "What's going on? Are we on track or not?"

Finally, on December 15, Democratic Party chairman Mike Tate broke the silence and announced that more than 500,000 signatures had been collected—and set a new goal of 720,277 signatures, 33 percent of the 2010 general election turnout.

What was happening behind the scenes between November 27 and December 15 was a catfight between web-enabled, grassroots "open" organizations and the state's traditional, hierarchical "closed" organization, a.k.a. the Democratic Party. Open groups were arguing for transparency in reporting the number of signatures gathered on the petitions. The closed Democratic Party worried that sharing the numbers would cause recall supporters to ease up and lose momentum.

Bryan Bliss, a spokesman for the open grassroots movement in Wisconsin, said, "I expressed my disagreement with hiding the numbers. A lot of grassroots support for recall is from people who are rebelling against the lack of accountability and transparency in the Walker administration. People don't like that. It's not a grassroots way to do things."

The future of America will be more grassroots and more open. Technology enables it, the next generation expects it, and the process of regeneration works best when systems are open, transparent, limber, and networked.

Corpus Christi, Texas, councilman David Loeb is a next-gener who has seen this in his community. Loeb has a boyish face, an earnest disposition, and a heart for what works. Early in his council career, the city wanted to support the local arts community and planned its inaugural Artwalk. Only 30 folks showed up. It was a lot of work for such a small turnout, so the city changed its approach. They engaged the local arts community to do the planning and promoting, and the city simply chipped in with support: map, printing, graphics, and transportation.

The event exploded. As Loeb sees it, Artwalk's popularity grew because the city gave up control.

Wikipedia works because anyone can post in their area of knowledge—and those who have more knowledge can edit those posts. It's an open, mutually reinforcing proposition, where you are both a contributor and a recipient. (And if you use Wikipedia, you should donate.)

This type of open-source software works because the product is free to anyone, and if you improve it in some way, you add your improvement to the database so that others can find it. Again: contributors and beneficiaries.

America is turning toward openness. Transparency. The days when a long-standing, central organization controls all the information are going the way of the Politburo. Thanks, WikiLeaks.

Regeneration requires collaboration. Collaboration requires trust. Trust requires openness and reciprocation.

The difference between countries that can sustain rapid growth

for many years or even decades and the many others that see

growth spurts fade quickly may be the level of inequality.

Andrew Berg and Jonathan Ostry

Question 3: Does a Middle Class Matter?

I grew up middle-class. Maybe you did, too. My dad worked second shift at a factory, and he was the primary breadwinner. Occasionally my mom worked as a substitute teacher, but mostly she looked after my brother and me, our home, and our grandma, who lived next door.

Middle class was burned into my identity. I was taught to be wary of rich people, and that middle-class people like us were morally superior. Still, I couldn't help noticing that rich people seemed to have more toys. Their families took vacations that required airplanes—to Disneyland, to the mountains to ski, to Europe. My family took vacations in an Oldsmobile to places like Mount Rushmore. Rich people had in-ground pools and belonged to the country club. Middle-class kids went to the local lake and belonged to 4-H clubs. Kids from rich families not only went to college, they drove there in their own cars. Kids from middle-class families sometimes went to college, and got dropped off in their parents' station wagons.

Thinking back, my childhood seems so . . . old-fashioned. Today, the idea that a sole breadwinner can work consistently at an American factory for 30 years and earn enough money to take vacations, send his kids to college, and retire comfortably seems as dated as a Polaroid photo. All brown and orange and pixelated.

Are my childhood memories really old-fashioned? Is it true that the middle-class upbringing that my parents provided me is less accessible to today's families? What does middle class mean, anyway? And does America's middle class matter, or is it another political turn of phrase thrown around during elections, like "small business" or "family values"?

Let's dig into this a little deeper.

When President Obama took office, he appointed the White House Task Force on the Middle Class. They consulted with economists, demographers, and other people with really large brains, trying to define middle class. Turns out, no standard definition exists. The report concludes:

> Middle-class families are defined by their aspirations more than their income. (The) report assumes that middle-class families aspire to home ownership, a car, college education for their children, health and retirement security, and occasional family vacations.[30]

So there you have it: America's middle class is defined by these six aspirations, which range in cost across the country:

(1) To own a home

---

30   *Annual Report of the White House Task Force on the Middle Class*, February 2010: www.whitehouse.gov/sites/default/files/microsites/100226-annual-report-middle-class. pdf (hereafter referred to as *ARMC*).

(2) To own a car

(3) To provide a college education for their kids

(4) To be "secure" in their health, e.g., to enjoy good health and adequate health care

(5) To be "secure" in their retirement, e.g., to live comfortably

(6) To take occasional family vacations

But here's the rub. When you look at average household incomes for married couples with two kids, the task force found, "It is more difficult now than in the past for many people to achieve middle-class status because prices for certain key goods—health care, college and housing—have gone up faster than incomes."

It's more expensive to be middle class.

Figure 3: Growth in Productivity and Real Median Family Income, 1947–2008

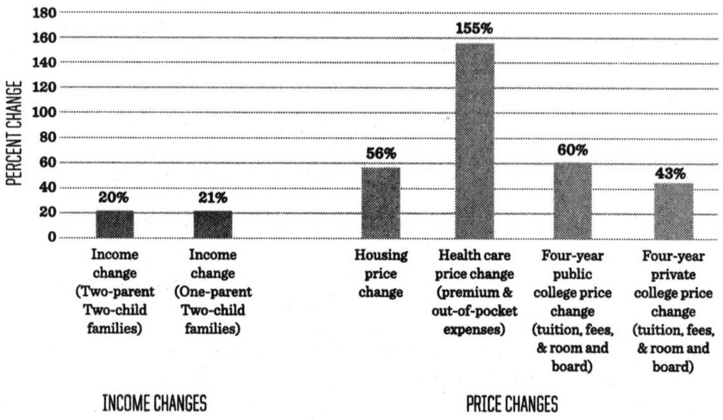

In his peak earning years, my dad earned $24,000 per year. That's $42,000 in today's dollars,[31] which would put my family in the lower quartile of today's middle class. But when I was growing up in the 1970s, we weren't in the lower quartile, we were in the middle of the pack. What happened?

Two things:

Beginning in about 1979, middle-class wages stagnated (see the solid line in figure 4), even though productivity (dotted line) continued to climb (*ARMC*, 3.) For the last 30 years, productivity increases have not

Figure 4: Changes in Median Family Income

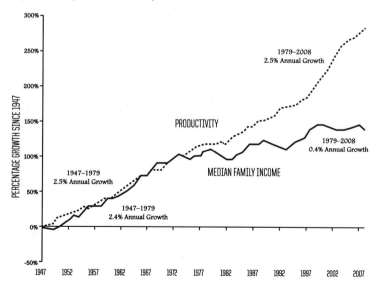

been distributed evenly. The rich really have been getting richer, at the expense of the middle class.

In America, nostalgia has a way of crowding out facts. So when politicians talk about the importance of the middle class, are they just trying to push our buttons, or does the middle class really matter? After all, there are many countries with wide gaps between rich and poor; are they at any real disadvantage?

Turns out, a middle class really does matter. *Really, really.* A strong middle class is an economic issue. And a social issue. And an issue of civilized societies. And not just to those who are in the middle class. Having a robust middle class is important to the poor, the middle class, *and the rich.*

First, there's the practical consideration: a thriving middle class can afford to send their kids to college, take family vacations, and buy homes and cars. All those transactions help turn America's economic wheel.

Venture capitalist Nick Hanauer explained it this way:

> In a capitalist economy the true job creators are middle class consumers. And taxing the rich to make investments that make the middle class grow and thrive is the single

shrewdest thing we can do for this middle class, the poor, and the rich.[32]

Henry Ford understood this. In 1914, he shocked America when he announced that all of his male factory workers would be paid $5 for an eight-hour shift. Previously, they had been paid $2.34 for nine hours' work.

Ford didn't double wages because he was philanthropic. He was acting in his own self-interest. By paying his people more, he was making his company one of the most attractive places to work, and he was creating a whole new class of folks who could afford to buy his cars. This bold economic stimulus was aimed squarely at the middle class.

---

32   You can read the transcript of Nick's speech and view his slides here: www.theatlantic.com/business/archive/2012/05/ here-is-the-full-inequality-speech-and-slideshow-that-was-too-hot-for-ted/257323/.

What impact would Henry Ford's economic stimulus have on today's working class?

To calculate, we start by adjusting 1914 dollars to current dollars. Ford paid his workers $5 for an eight-hour day in 1914. Adjusted for 2013 dollars, that's equivalent to $114.54 per eight-hour shift, or $14.32 per hour. As this book goes to print, the median minimum wage is $7.25 Therefore Ford's 1914 wages were 65 percent higher than America's current minimum wage.[33]

Yes, having a healthy middle class is good for the American economy. But it's good for much, much more. In countries and states that have large, gaping inequalities between rich and poor—in other words, where there is not a robust middle class—research shows a whole host of social and health problems crop up: a larger imprisoned population, higher rates of violence, more teenage pregnancies, earlier death, higher infant mortality, lower literacy, more obesity, worse mental health, and so on.[34]

Sounds charming, doesn't it?

It should also sound familiar.

---

33   Again, I use the CPI Index, and the online calculator offered at www.stats.arep-pim.com/calc/calc_usdlrxdeflxcpi.php.

34   Richard Wilkinson and Kate Pickett, *The Spirit Level: Why Greater Equality Makes Societies Stronger* (New York: Bloomsbury Press, 2009), 174 (hereafter cited in text as SL).

Compared to other countries, the United States is joined only by the United Kingdom and Portugal as being *the most unequal* (SL 5–7). We have far more super-rich and super-poor. We have a smaller middle class. And because of that, we suffer.

The conclusion? If we want a healthy society—for our rich and our poor and everyone in between—we need greater income equality. In other words, we need a robust middle class.

So, a critical follow-up question for America's regeneration is this: how will our middle class make a comeback? How can they regain their lost decades and get back to within an arm's reach of achieving those six aspirations: owning a home and car, putting their kids through college, securing adequate health care and retirement benefits, and taking the occasional family vacation?

This is evolving into much more than an economic issue. It's becoming political. Mitch Daniels, the former Republican governor of Indiana, challenged his party's major funders to recognize the importance of the upward mobility that enables the middle class:

> We must display a heart for every American, and a special
> passion for those still on the first rung of life's ladder.
> Upward mobility from the bottom is the crux of the
> American promise, and the stagnation of the middle class
> is in fact becoming a problem, on any fair reading of the

facts. Our main task is not to see that people of great wealth add to it, but that those without much money have a greater chance to earn some.[35]

A robust middle class is as American as apple pie. When our middle class is strong, our income equality is greater. When America is more equal, our social and health challenges subside. We become a more civilized society, for the poor, the middle class, *and* the wealthy.

---

35   Mitch Daniels, speech to Ronald Reagan Centennial Dinner, Conservative Political Action Conference (CPAC), Washington, DC, February 11, 2011. Full transcript, http://
dailycaller.com/2011/02/11/full-text-mitch-daniels-speech-to-cpac/, accessed November
24, 2012, audio recording, www.youtube.com/watch?v=9vJ9mcwQ_oI, accessed November
24, 2012.

The scaling process is no longer happening in the US. And as long as that's the case, plowing capital into young companies that build their factories elsewhere will continue to yield a bad return in terms of American jobs.

Andy Grove

Question 4: JOBS: What's It Gonna Take?

Several months ago, my mother decided to sell her condo but listed it well above the price I felt was reasonable. To help adjust her expectations, I calculated the sale price per square foot of all the condos that had sold in her zip code in the last 12 months. Then I figured her home's square footage and explained, "Based on the market, your condo should sell for about $138,000."

This was considerably lower than her asking price. But Mom, at 85, lives in her own universe. And she's stubborn. She defended her price: "I have a built-in china cabinet, and a screened-in porch. How many of those condos had those things?"

I countered, "No one has china anymore. And your porch isn't up to code."

She wasn't buying my argument: *that her condo wasn't worth what she wanted; it was worth what the buyer was willing to pay for it.*[36]

How does this relate to jobs?

We're not going to get Americans back to work simply because we want to.

Americans will get back to work when we're making stuff that other people want to buy for a price that can support the jobs. Our nostalgia

---

36   Mom eventually sold her condo for $140,000.

for belching smokestacks and thousand-job economic deals must be set aside like a well-worn child's book and replaced with a crisp new textbook that addresses our current and future economic realities.

Here are three realities that a regenerated economy must address:

{1}

The long job is dead.

How long have you had your current job?

A year? Two years? Five? Ten?

In the United States, the average worker's tenure is 4.4 years. You read that right; there's a dot between the fours. Most American women will have 10.7 jobs in their careers; men will have 11.4.[37]

In contrast, when my dad retired from the West Bend Company in 1989, he'd worked there for 33 years. You read that right; there was *no dot* between the threes.

People who study such things would say that my dad had a "long job," and America's current workforce experiences "short jobs" or "gigs."

---

37   Anya Kamenetz, "The Four Year Career," *Fast Company*, January 12, 2012, www.fastcompany.com/1802731/four-year-career, accessed January 25, 2012.

What's interesting is how many institutions—government, the US Chamber of Commerce, health insurance companies, and others—just don't get it.

When I visited[38] the White House a couple of years ago, we saw four huge posters hanging from the front of the US Chamber of Commerce building, which faces the White House.

The four posters had one letter on each of them, and together they spelled J-O-B-S.

No doubt, the US Chamber is playing to Americans' nostalgia for long jobs. But their call for J-O-B-S masks the truth: the chamber's members, like many American employers, don't support long jobs anymore. They lay off millions during each recession; rely increasingly on part-timers, independent contractors, and consultants; and in many ways prefer short-term employees. They're cheaper. They don't require health care coverage. Even CEOs have short shelf lives.

Long jobs have been gone for a long time. But it's not just tenure that's changed; the workforce has changed, too.

Our next generation of American workers may like the financial security of a long job, but many relish the variety that our current "gig economy" offers. It's not just Gen Xers and Millennials who work in

---

38   By "visit" I mean I had my picture taken out front.

the gig economy. Increasingly, Baby Boomers are joining it, too. Kelly Staffing estimates that more than two-thirds of all free agents are Baby Boomers or Silents.

Baratunde Thurston is the digital director for the *Onion*, the author of *How to Be Black*, and a stand-up comedian. He works squarely in the gig economy, and he's not sympathetic toward people who long for the good ol' days.

"I was talking to some documentary filmmakers at a conference, and they all just talk about loss, the loss of a model," Thurston says. "I can empathize. But I'm not upset that the model is dying. The milkman is dead, but we drink more milk than ever. Do we really want to return to a world of just three broadcast channels?"

And that's a critical point. There's a lot of work to be done in this country. And it's time for America to stop lamenting how we used to do that work, and embrace how we currently do it.

If we can accept and embrace the gig economy, we can also think more creatively about how to nurture and support the economy we have, not the one we remember.

For example, how can freelancers get access to affordable health insurance? As it is, many people stay in long jobs for the benefits. This hurts everyone. Someone with a great business idea won't take the risk to start her own company because she can't afford to lose her health insurance. And long-suffering long jobbers who would really like to leave their current organization feel trapped. Many Baby Boomers admit this applies to them. A friend recently barked at me, "Want to get more Millennials into the workplace? Give all of us Boomers affordable health insurance, and we'd leave in a snap!"

Coupling health insurance with long jobs has been a drag on America for a long time; it's made health care more expensive for everyone, especially employers. And it's dampened the innovation economy that just wants to spread its wings and fly.

How else can we support those who work and produce and add value and create prosperity in the gig economy?

» We can turn old warehouses into coworking spaces like NextSpace in California.[39]

» We can resurrect the guild model, where creatives join together in a contemporary mash-up of trade union + cartel + membership society.

» We can finally make entrepreneurship a core part of the American education curriculum.

---

39   Some of this chapter is based on an article I wrote for *Madison Magazine* that appeared in the March 2012 issue, www.madisonmagazine.com/Madison-Magazine/March-2012/The-Future-of-Work-The-Long-Job-is-Dead-the-Gig-Economy-is-Here/.

The long job is dead. Long live the gig economy.

{2}

We need entrepreneurial support organizations.

For almost 30 years in Littleton, Colorado, an experiment has been taking shape. In 1987 Chris Gibbons, the city's economic development director, decided that traditional economic development, that is, trying to lure very large companies with tax breaks, was unsustainable. So Gibbons and his posse tried something different, to work with local businesses to develop good jobs. They consistently refined their approach and eventually landed on the recipe that's today called "economic gardening."[40]

Economic gardening is grounded in these ideas:

(1) It's more effective to keep and grow the companies you have than try to attract new ones.

(2) Small businesses are important, and some are more important than others. The important ones are "gazelles," startups that have the ability to grow quickly.

---

40   Christian Gibbons, "Economic Gardening: An Entrepreneurial Approach to Economic Development," www.littletongov.org/bia/economicgardening/, accessed November 9, 2012.

(3) Gazelles usually meet the following criteria:

» They have wacky founders.

» They have the will and capacity to be a fast-growing business.

» They surf on the edge of structure and chaos.

Gazelles need "entrepreneurial support organizations" to provide:

» Information and data that can be used to develop business plans, including marketing plans, competitive intelligence, industry trends, new product tracking, legislative research, and more

» Training in advanced management techniques

» Quality-of-life projects like public parks, trails, and community festivals. Says Gibbons, "In the New Economy, where new wealth and jobs are being created by knowledge firms, creating a community that is attractive to entrepreneurs and the talent they hire is as important as natural resources and heavy rail were to Old Economy companies."

» Connections to trade associations, think tanks, academic institutions, and similar companies[41]

---

41   Ibid.

What does it take to grow gazelles, and why does it really matter?

The Edward Lowe Foundation has discovered that "second stage growth entrepreneurs" (a definition that includes gazelles and companies that have steady but less dramatic growth) represent a small slice (10.9%) of US companies but account for 36.2 percent of jobs and 38.6 percent of sales.[42] In other words, these small but mighty companies punch above their weight class, providing three times more jobs and sales than their market share.

Mark Lange, the former executive director of the Edward Lowe Foundation, says, "It's important to treat these growth entrepreneurs differently than small businesses. Communities need to identify their second-stage companies and make sure services and resources are in place to help them continue to grow." Yet in most communities traditional chambers of commerce and economic development organizations are not retooling to help stage two companies.

If we want to create jobs and prosperity in America, we have to accept the fact that all businesses are important, but some are more important than others.

---

42   "The Significance of Second Stage," Edward Lowe Foundation, http://edward-lowe.org/edlowenetwp/wp-content/themes/implementprogram/downloads/infosheets/SecondStage.pdf, accessed November 29, 2012.

{3}

Meet manufacturing's geeky younger brother, the maker.

You've probably read many stories about how American manufacturing is dead. This is simply not true. Large-scale, mass-produced crap may be in decline, but the spirit of manufacturing has been reincarnated across the country in makers, a subculture of do-it-yourselfers powered by technology who see life through open-source lenses.

Their haunts are local makerspaces, a.k.a. hackerspaces, where they learn and experiment with robotics, electronics, metalworking, woodworking, and more. Best part? They can fabricate their inventions on the spot using 3D printers, lathes, and the kind of machinery that you and I used to see in shop classes but now see mostly on TV shows like *Mythbusters*.

Today's makers build beautiful lines of code and helpful apps. They bandage handmade cheeses. They run small organic farms. They bake delicious breads, design stunning graphics, and manufacture delightful gadgets. They sell their stuff on Etsy.

Makers take pride in their work. They are not motivated by how much they can make; they take pride in how well things are made and how long they will last.

Companies like San Francisco bag maker Timbuk2 embody the maker ethos, blending the speed of technology and digitization (go online and design your bag to your own unique tastes) with the workmanship and durability of something that's built to last. I own several Timbuk2 bags. *They're awesome.* And no one else has one just like mine.

Stormy Kromer, the mercantile that's been building and selling iconic wool hats since the early 1900s, puts a lifetime guarantee on their products. Their hats are sewn in Michigan by hand. And every part of the Stormy Kromer brand has that unmistakable upper-Midwestern sensibility. Ya der hey.

This is not just a brand affectation. Makers are deeply connected to their place. Stormy Kromer isn't going to leave Michigan. America's first farm-to-table restaurant, Berkeley's Chez Panisse, isn't going to open restaurants in Vegas and NYC. Makers are investors in their local economies, creating jobs and prosperity for their neighbors and friends.

Phil Libin, CEO of software maker Evernote, wrote about his company's makerish commitment to building things that endure in his blog post of July 13, 2011:

> Remember that scene in The Social Network when Sean Parker says, "A million dollars isn't cool, you know what's cool? A billion dollars"?

Well, we don't think a billion dollars is all that cool either. You know what's really cool? Making a hundred-year company. That's a pretty big deal; not many companies make it anywhere close, but we sort of signed up for the task when we started talking about earning your lifetime trust. You plan on living a long time, right?

So when we make any big decision, whether in fund-raising, or product design, or partnership strategy, we ask, "Would this make it more or less likely that we'll be around in a hundred years?" and if the answer is less we don't do it.[43]

The takeaway is this: Americans will always make things, but the things they will make will have greater variety (digital and physical, products and services), serve more distinct niches (versus the mass market), and reemphasize design, quality, and durability.

Someone once quipped that American women keep the hairstyle from the period of their lives when they felt most attractive. In America, we seem to be attached to the economic policies from our most prosperous periods. But maybe it's time to trade in that 1970s bob for a more contemporary razor cut. For regeneration to reach its potential with the American economy, we don't need drastic overhaul, we just need

---

43   Phil Libin, "Evernote Gets $50 Million in Funding, Plus an FAQ," http://blog. evernote.com/blog/2011/07/13/evernote-gets-50-million-in-funding-with-faq/, accessed November 11, 2012.

policies and institutions to catch up to how things are today, instead of trying to re-create the economy that once was.

Too much and for too long, we seem to have surrendered personal

excellence and community values in the mere accumulation of

material things. Our gross national product ... counts air pollution

and cigarette advertising, and ambulances to clear our highways of

carnage. Yet the gross national product does not allow for the health

of our children, the quality of their education or the joy of their

play. It does not include the beauty of our poetry or the strength of

our marriages, the intelligence of our public debate or the integrity

of our public officials ... It measures everything in short, except

that which makes life worthwhile. And it can tell us everything

about America except why we are proud that we are Americans.

Robert F. Kennedy

Question 5: What's the Point of America?

You probably weren't alive in 1928, but here's a little rundown of what life was like. Americans circa 1928:

» Didn't own their home; they rented a room or a small apartment or house.

» Didn't own a car; they got around on foot or in larger cities via trolley or bus.

» Didn't have air-conditioning.

» Had one or two outfits in their tiny little closets.

» Had a single pair of shoes.

» Took a bath once a week, usually on Saturday night.

Basically, they lived lives of poverty. Like nuns. And this was *before* the Great Depression! In 1928, Herbert Hoover's campaign slogan, "A chicken in every pot, and a car in every garage,"[44] was truly aspirational.

Today, a chicken in every pot seems quaint. Who hasn't had chicken this week? Americans eat 12 ounces of meat a day.[45]

---

44   Herbert Hoover never actually said this. The Republican National Committee is credited with attributing it to Hoover's presidential campaign.

45   "The State of Food and Agriculture: Livestock in the Balance," Food and Agriculture Organization of the United Nations (2009), 136, www.fao.org/docrep/012/i0680e/i0680e.pdf, accessed November 24, 2012.

And what about a car in every garage? A friend recently emailed to say that she and her husband, a car fanatic, were moving after years of searching for a new house. "We finally found a large garage with a house attached to it," Linda joked.

America has come a long way since '28, when a chicken in every pot and a car in every garage seemed like hyperbole.

We have achieved those goals.

And surpassed them.

And it's making us miserable.

A National Cancer Institute study of 500,000 Americans found that people who eat four ounces of red meat or processed meat every day were 30 percent more likely to die in the 10 years of the study than those who ate five ounces of red meat or less per week.

And a happiness study found that commuting to work is the single daily activity most injurious to happiness. Time in our cars doesn't just make us miserable; it's also unraveling the threads that bind us together. In his book *Bowling Alone*, Harvard professor Robert Putnam writes:

> Each additional ten minutes in daily commuting time cuts involvement in community affairs by 10 percent—fewer public meetings attended, fewer committees chaired, fewer

petitions signed, fewer church services, less volunteering, and so on. In fact, although commuting time is not quite as powerful an influence on civic involvement as education, it is more important than any other demographic factor.[46]

A chicken in every pot and a car in every garage seemed like a great idea at the time, but are we happier? Are we healthier? Are we a better country because of it?

Public health professionals Richard Wilkinson and Kate Pickett lay our challenge before us:

> For the vast majority of people in affluent countries, the difficulties of life are no longer about filling our stomachs, having clean water, and keeping warm. Most of us now want to eat less, not more. And, for the first time in history, the poor are—on average—fatter than the rich. Economic growth, for so long the great engine of progress, has, in the rich countries, largely finished its work. Not only have measures of well-being and happiness ceased to rise with economic growth, but as affluent societies have grown richer, there have been long-term rises in rates of anxiety, depression and numerous other social problems . . . Having come to the end of what material living standards can offer,

---

46   Robert Putnam, *Bowling Alone: The Collapse and Revival of American Community* (New York: Simon & Schuster, 2000), 213.

we are the first generation to have to find other ways of improving the real quality of life (SL 29).

That last phrase burns my eyes: *We are the first generation to have to find other ways of improving the real quality of life.*

What's the point of being an American after we've achieved fat bellies and so many material possessions that we have to rent storage spaces?

This is a critical question for our regeneration. Because if the answer is not bigger, fatter, more-of-the-same, what is it?

For guidance, let's return to America's mission statement, our Declaration of Independence:

> We hold these truths to be self-evident, that all Men are created equal, that they are endowed by their Creator with certain unalienable Rights, that among these are Life, Liberty, and the pursuit of Happiness.

Notice that our founding fathers never said, "All Americans will be rich!" Or, "We'll become so fat, we'll need bariatric surgery!" Their aim wasn't to guarantee an *outcome*; they wanted to guarantee *an equal chance* at a good outcome.

But Americans have forgotten this. And here's why. Those of us who experienced the great prosperity of America's recent spring-summer-fall cycle (1946–2000) have inadvertently rewritten our declaration in our collective consciousness. We have substituted "material possessions" for "happiness."

Who can blame us? For two, almost three generations, Americans have been sitting at the equivalent of a giant, national economic craps table, placing our bets. And we've been winning big. Every time.

Here's how I see it.

Our grandparents, everyday folks who got called into a war, fought with courage and were victorious, came back to America, placed a few bets at the economic craps table . . . and won big. A new house. The suburbs. Brand-new appliances. They started winning consistently: wall-to-wall carpeting, a shiny new car, job security, pensions.

As my 91-year-old friend Betty Techman told me, "If you couldn't make money after the war, you weren't trying!"

The GIs raised their Baby Boomer kids at the same craps table, placing bets and again, mostly winning. Second homes. Luxury vacations. College for the kids. An entire generation of Americans started to believe that playing craps—and winning—was what it meant to be an American. They couldn't help themselves; it was the reality of their lives.

Except for this one tiny problem. When America headed into fall (1980–2000), the tables started to turn. Bets that had always been good weren't paying off consistently. Jobs went overseas—and job security went with them. A good education no longer guaranteed a good job. Home values stopped endlessly increasing. Credit card rates didn't stay low. The odds turned against us.

So now, in winter we find ourselves in an economic hangover. We are a nation of glassy-eyed, up-all-night gamblers who've been sitting at the craps table for so long, on such a bodacious winning streak, that many of us don't know who we are or how we got here.

It's time to reboot. To remember.

The point of America is laid out clearly. We have the rights to life, liberty, and the pursuit of happiness. But for two generations, economic expansion—all the stuff that money can buy—has been happiness's surrogate. And we've now learned it was the wrong surrogate. It's made us sicker. And less happy. And less resilient.

So what does life, liberty, and the pursuit of happiness mean today, if our economic measuring sticks are insufficient?

Many cities, states, and countries are asking these same questions. Even Federal Reserve chairman Ben Bernanke is asking, insisting that the purpose of economics is to enhance happiness's sister, well-being:

As we think about new directions for economic measurement, we might start by reminding ourselves of the purpose of economics. Textbooks describe economics as the study of the allocation of scarce resources. That definition may indeed be the "what," but it certainly is not the "why." The ultimate purpose of economics, of course, is to understand and promote the enhancement of well-being. Economic measurement accordingly must encompass measures of well-being and its determinants.[47]

America is not the first country to enter the discussion about well-being's role in the economy. But our willingness to ask—to self-reflect—is an important signal to the rest of the world that an economic yardstick may be insufficient to measure a country's progress.

And as we ask these courageous questions, which for so long had unquestionable, obvious responses, we do something critically important for our regeneration. We make room. We clear the air. We create space for new ideas, new voices, and unknown outcomes. We admit that we may have pursued the wrong path.

And when we know better, we can do better.

---

47   Ben Bernanke, "Economic Measurement," speech delivered at the 32nd General Conference of the International Association for Research in Income and Wealth (Cambridge, MA, August 6, 2012), www.federalreserve.gov/newsevents/speech/bernanke20120806a.htm.

When you study the history of rights, you begin with the
Magna Carta, which was about the rights of white, English,
noble males. With the Declaration of Independence, rights
were expanded to all land-owning white males.

Nearly a century later, we moved to the emancipation
of slaves, and during the beginnings of this century, to
suffrage, giving the right to women to vote.

Then the pace picks up with the Civil Rights Act of 1964, and then
in 1973, the Endangered Species Act. For the first time, the right
of other species and organisms to exist was recognized. We have
essentially "declared" that Homo sapiens are part of the web of life.

Thus, if Thomas Jefferson were with us today, he would be calling
for a Declaration of Interdependence which recognizes that our
ability to pursue wealth, health, and happiness is dependent on
other forms of life, that the rights of one species are linked to
the rights of others and none should suffer remote tyranny.

William McDonough, 1993

Question 6: What Commitment Are We Willing to Make to Our Planet?

At the Interstate 80 rest area outside of Adair, Iowa, they've installed a new monument: five pillars lead from the parking lot to the shelter, each one representing Iowa's levels of topsoil over time. The first pillar closest to the parking lot is labeled "1850." In that year Iowa had 14–16 inches of topsoil. Fast-forward to the last pillar; today Iowa has 6–8 inches of topsoil.

No big deal, right?

It's just dirt.

Wrong.

It takes 500 years to replace one inch of topsoil.[48] At this rate Iowa would need 3,000 to 5,000 years to replace what's been lost in less than 200 years. Why is the soil eroding at such a fast clip? Development is part of it; the growth of Des Moines suburbs in the last 20 years are proof of that. But many of the farming methods we use to grow our food, such as tilling, are eliminating the soil in which we grow it.

Seems that no matter where you turn, there's evidence that our modern American lifestyle is depleting our planet.

---

48   David R. Montgomery, Dirt: *The Erosion of Civilizations* (Berkeley: University of California Press, 2007), p. 147.

Just how badly are we screwing things up?

» *Our air.* June 2012 was the 328th consecutive month in which the temperature of the entire globe exceeded the 20th-century average. The odds of that occurring by simple chance are 3.7 x 1,099, a number considerably larger than the number of stars in the universe.[49]

» *Our water.* The world's oceans now have 450 dead zones. Dead zones are caused primarily by nitrogen and phosphorous runoff from farm fields, which kills bottom-dwelling sea creatures like crabs, disrupting the food chain and sending predators up higher, into warmer waters. Warmer temperatures prevent proper growth of species' reproductive organs and slow reproduction. The world's largest dead zone, the Baltic Sea, has lost about 30 percent of available food energy, crippling the fishing industry. And because all of our water systems are linked, most of the world's drinking water now includes trace amounts of pharmaceuticals and steroids like Viagra, birth control drugs, Valium, antipsychotics, and the like.[50]

---

49   Bill McKibben, "Global Warming's Terrifying New Math," *Rolling Stone*, July 19, 2012, www.rollingstone.com/politics/news/global-warmings-terrifying-new-math-20120719, accessed November 25, 2012.

50   Marla Cone, "Traces of Prescription Drugs Found in Southland Aquifers," *Los Angeles Times*, January 30, 2006, http://articles.latimes.com/print/2006/jan/30/local/me-drugs30, accessed November 28, 2012.

» *Our weather.* If you live along a coastline, you know it's getting more and more expensive to insure your house. That's because insurance companies—historically some of the most profitable companies on the planet (Warren Buffett holds a lot of these stocks)—are freaking out about climate change. They expect that our storms will become more severe and more frequent. Recent history is proving them right: 20 of the 30 most expensive insured catastrophes worldwide from 1970 to 2011 have occurred since 2001, and all but one (9/11) were natural disasters.[51]

At this rate our kids will have arid air and soil, lifeless oceans, and storms of increasing frequency and intensity.

Armageddon may be coming by our own hand.

How did we get to this point?

Throughout history, God and Creation (or "the environment") have always battled for the attention of our better angels. In 1606, the First Charter of Virginia was crafted, to incorporate Jamestown. Its official mission was to propagate Christianity, but only 3 percent of the 3,805 words in the document refer to it. The other 97 percent outlined how the colonists might pillage "all the Lands, Woods, Soul, Grounds, Havens, Ports, Rivers, Mines, Minerals, Marshes, Waters, Fishing,

---

51   Erwann Michel-Kerjan and Howard Kunreuther, "Paying for Future Catastrophes," *New York Times*, November 24, 2012, www.nytimes.com/2012/11/25/opinion/sunday/paying-for-future-catastrophes.html?_r=0, accessed November 26, 2012.

Commodities," using options including but not limited to "dig, mine, and search for all Manner of Mines of Gold, Silver, and Copper."

America has always put God on its masthead, but in the fine print, we've been treating his creation—land, air, water, people, plants, and so on—with disregard.

I can let us off the hook for the first while; we didn't know better. Most Americans at the founding of our country believed that nature would be endlessly abundant and that upward economic growth was infinite. But of course, America had fewer people then. And less-intensive farming methods. And suppliers and consumers lived shoulder to shoulder, which brought more transparency to transactions. A farmer couldn't just dump a bunch of waste into a stream that his neighbors used for drinking water.

Over time, we've lost touch with nature and have come to treat it as a system to be controlled or, worse, looted. Modern industrialism spawned a "take-make-waste" economic system: we take natural resources like water to make textiles that consumers buy and eventually discard or waste.

Our take-make-waste system leaves our planet more polluted. For example, just one Patagonia R2® jacket requires 135 liters of water, enough to meet the daily needs (three glasses a day) of 45 people. Its journey from origin to warehouse generates nearly 20 pounds of carbon dioxide, 24 times the weight of the finished product, leaving behind two-thirds its weight in waste. Patagonia admits, "This jacket comes with an environmental cost higher than its price." [52]

Now consider that the average US consumer throws away 68 pounds of clothing and fabrics each year, the weight of a ten-year-old kid.

But nature is not simply the victim of our recklessness. Nature is also our teacher, showing us the way out and through the ecological crisis we are facing.

In 2004, I visited Hawaii as a guest of Honolulu mayor Jeremy Harris, a biologist. I was impressed by Mayor Harris's and other elected officials' care and respect for the environment. As one example, they put strict limits on the number of guests who could visit Hanauma Bay, one of the most gorgeous coral bays in the world. Before entering the area, all tourists have to watch a short film that teaches them how to respect the coral and animals, and how to properly discard their own trash. And on Tuesdays, the bay is completely closed, giving it a chance to rest and recuperate.

In nature, the moment you stop harming, the system begins to repair itself.

---

52   Patagonia, "Don't Buy This Jacket, Black Friday and the New York Times," November 25, 2011 www.thecleanestline.com/2011/11/dont-buy-this-jacket-black-friday-and-the-new-york-times.html, accessed on November 29, 2012.

Some countries have broader measures to balance the relationship between man and nature.

In Ecuador in 2008, the citizens voted in a referendum to include earth rights in their constitution. Rather than treating nature as property, their laws acknowledge that nature in all its life forms has the right to exist, persist, maintain, and regenerate its vital cycles. And the Ecuadorian people have the legal authority to enforce these rights on behalf of ecosystems.

In 2011, Bolivia went even further, establishing 11 new rights for Earth. Vice President Alvaro García Linear calls the law historic: "It establishes a new relationship between man and nature, the harmony of which must be preserved as a guarantee of its regeneration."

Here in America, we are still of the mind that the environment is ours to pillage. But this just doesn't square with my Christian upbringing. I was taught that God first created the heavens and the earth. Adam and Eve came last and were charged by God with caring for His creation, not decimating it.

Our kids and grandkids who will still be alive when spring comes again have a true urgency to save our planet. The number of students taking classes in environmental science and bioethics is shooting through the roof. And it's no wonder. Their whole lives, our next generation has seen images of barges looking for a place to dump their waste, rivers poisoned by factory runoff, birds and fish killed by oil spills, and polar bears going extinct.

What our next generation knows—and we would all be wise to acknowledge—is that there is no Planet B.

You've asked me to tell you of the Great Turning

Of how we saved the world from disaster.

The answer is both simple and complex.

We turned.

Christine Fry, "The Great Turning

PART FOUR: WHEN SPRING COMES AGAIN

For two years as I've been writing this book, I've been fretting about this moment.

We've come to the last chapter and you're wondering, "So what, Rebecca? What can I do about all this?" Americans are naturally inclined to take action. We want to *do* something.

Advice like, "Vote," or "Research the issues" feels hollow to me, and I suspect it would feel hollow to you, too.

And then it hit me.

If we want to know how to turn from winter to spring, we should go to the guru, the most experienced seasonal sensei, *nature herself.*

Nature has been cycling through seasons for eons, adjusting as she goes. She has withstood an ice age, natural disasters of all kinds, and is now facing climate change. How does nature persist?

Nature is an open system, constantly taking in new information and stimuli and adjusting accordingly. America is also an open system. A democracy. A (more or less) free market. Nature and open systems theory teach us that for America to adapt and endure, we must work in alignment with four powerful principles:

» Emergent properties

» Balance

» Adaptation

» Nested holons[53] and bottom-up change

Here's a brief interpretation of each principle, followed by ideas to take action for regeneration.

Principle #1: Emergent properties

When you add two individual things together and get something new and unexpected, you have developed emergent properties. Combining peanut butter and chocolate is my favorite low-tech example; the mad genius who invented peanut butter cups should be canonized.

A nerdier example is blending hydrogen and oxygen. Separately, both are gases. But when you combine two parts hydrogen with one part oxygen, the compound changes from gas to water. The emergent property created by two gases is wetness.

Amazing.

Nature has the ability to produce millions of emergent properties. You are a perfect example. That's right, *you*. There will never be another human exactly like you. Your parents' unique genetic material

---

53   If you've never heard of this word "holon" before, don't freak. Most people haven't heard of it. But it's a really cool concept, so stick with me.

combined and formed a completely new and dynamic emergent property: you.

How can you put the principle of emergent properties to work during regeneration?

****

Be open to building relationships with
people who are different from you.

****

America's increasing diversity and lengthening life span means you'll be working with fewer Caucasians and more Latinos, Asian Americans, African Americans, and older folks. At work, former competitors might become allies. In communities, groups of different faiths will join together and become powerful forces for change. Politically, we will see a new breed of leader emerge: one who is able to work with both Democrats *and* Republicans. How's that for an unexpected emergent property?

If you are open to moving beyond your comfy, homogenous cocoon and joining forces with others, you have a powerful opportunity to create unexpected and innovative emergent properties.

****

Share. Be willing to add your little bit of good to that of others.

****

If you spend any time on college campuses, you see kids sharing their lecture notes, sharing ideas, and working in teams. They're also into car sharing and tool sharing—they are the innovators behind the sharing economy. They have the right idea. America's "rugged individualism" story line is a myth. None of us could go for long without assistance from others. So reach out. Share. Build on others' good ideas and don't hide your own. We need all the good you can do.

Principle #2: Balance

Like a thermostat that regulates the temperature in your house, nature has a "set point" for optimal performance, and it continually monitors conditions and adapts to stay in balance.

Your body is a phenomenal example of this, maintaining its temperature, respiration, heartbeat, and cellular function without any of your conscious attention. If you inhale an airborne germ, your body produces a sneeze to eject it. When your body produces a strange cellular deviation called cancer, it mobilizes a chain reaction of responses to fight and kill the deviation before it replicates. Your body works hard to maintain balance and health.

America also has a set point: our values. As a society, we believe that America works best when freedom, equality, and justice are optimized for all of us. And when America becomes aware of imbalances, we recalibrate.

Take equality as an example. In the arc of our history—from the Civil War and Reconstruction to voting rights to the Lilly Ledbetter Fair Pay Act and now marriage equality for gays and lesbians—America continually resets toward more equality for more people. We are always moving closer to our values, our set point.

America is now imbalanced. Greater wealth is concentrating in the hands of fewer people. And America, an open, democratic system, is responding. Occupy Wall Street, President Obama's reelection, the public's favor for higher taxes for the wealthy—all are signals of America working to rebalance.

Here is one powerful way to leverage the principle of balance during regeneration:

****

Take a stand for freedom, equality, and justice
even if the issues don't directly benefit you.

****

In a redwood forest, all the trees' root systems are connected and work together to get enough water to all the trees. Miraculously, when one tree has had enough water, it stops drawing more water up its own trunk and instead diverts water through its underground root system to other trees that are still thirsty. By working together, the redwoods get the most water to the most trees.

During regeneration, some parts must mobilize for imbalances in a single part. Here are two examples:

Warren Buffett, America's famous billionaire, favors higher taxes for the rich. He doesn't think it's fair that his secretary pays more in taxes than he does. Mr. Buffett is not working in his own short-term self-interest; he's working in America's best long-term interest. When America is fairer toward all, our system is in better balance and our country works better for more people.

At gay pride parades, the group that gets the most whoops and hollers from the crowd is PFLAG, Parents and Friends of Lesbians and Gays. These people aren't gay themselves, but they have kids and loved ones who are, and they march to demonstrate their support.

Like the redwoods, Warren Buffett and PFLAG members are working not directly for themselves, but for the good of the whole.

Principle #3: Adaptation

The Audubon Society notes that in the last 40 years, more than half of all North American birds have moved north by an average of 35 miles. This, they speculate, is the birds' response to global warming. As climates have changed (Texas is in its 10th year of drought), birds move north to stay comfortable.

This is a simple example of how a species adapts to challenges.

In our current regenerative period, entire classes of people are readjusting to the new normal. The middle class is watching every dollar because of job insecurity. College kids are moving home after graduation because they can't find jobs or afford to live in expensive cities. The sharing economy—from Zipcar to the Oakland library that loans lawn and garden equipment—is taking root as a new generation of consumers question their need to own cars, tools, and gadgets.

Americans are creating a new normal, like our avian friends, to deal with a challenge to our ecosystem.

Here are some ideas to act on the principle of adaptation:

★★★★

Put on your own oxygen mask before assisting others.
Don't wait for someone else to do it for you.

★★★★

During this period of regeneration, you are going to have to take greater responsibility for yourself, especially your health and financial well-being. No matter how you slice it, I just don't see American policy moving in the direction of more entitlements for more Americans. We are entering a period where self-reliance will be a battle cry. You will be asked to step up and save more, and be advocates and practitioners of your own health—both financial and physical.

Now I know some of you may be saying, "But Rebecca, I can't do that! I'm already living on a shoestring." If that's true, I'd better not come to your house and find cable TV, junk food (which is more expensive per calorie than fresh fruits and vegetables), a closet full of rarely worn clothes, a new car, rent or a mortgage you can't afford, or other signs of silly spending.

Start by sacrificing whatever is not needed (cable, iPhone upgrades, eating out, etc.) to take care of yourself and those you love. To be prosperous in the new normal, most of us will need more education, more job training, and a larger safety cushion. So please, *please* save more money for these things. (I know, I feel like your parent writing this, but it's true.) In the near term, each of us will have to take more accountability for our own financial welfare.[54] We'll have to pay more to put our kids through school. We'll have to pay more for health care,

---

54   I am not being paid to endorse her book, but I really like the advice Suze Orman offers in her book *The Money Class*, because it's aligned with America's current winter-to-spring cycle.

and we'll need more savings to live comfortably in retirement. Start with yourself.

★★★★

If you're asked to do something you've never done before,
you're probably on the right path.

★★★★

Most of us alive at this moment have had a pretty stable ride in America to this point. We knew what to expect, and when. Now, our stability has been kicked out from underneath us. So the habits and behaviors that got you to winter are not the same ones you'll need during regeneration. The same rules simply don't apply. So, if you're out of your comfort zone, that's probably exactly where you need to be to adapt. Everyone's uncomfortable in winter. Those who can adapt will be big winners when spring comes again.

★★★★

Stay open.
Be willing to be wrong and curious enough to get smarter.

★★★★

Remember the book and movie *Moneyball*? A baseball nerd discovers that traditional statistics like hitting percentage and RBIs don't predict a team's success. Instead, he discovers an overlooked statistic, on-base percentage, which is more predictive of winning.

The Oakland As become the first team to adopt this strategy. But it's painful. Hitters are trained to hit. They want to get singles and doubles and triples. Now they have to learn to hold back, that getting walked is as valuable as hitting a single.

Players, managers, and other teams thought the As were crazy. Until they started winning. Until the ball club with the lowest payroll started beating teams that were believed to be superior.

The willingness of the Oakland As to be open to predictive data and then adjust their entire ball club's strategy toward that data is a compelling example of how to stay open and agile. Regeneration demands this.

****

Keep score differently.

****

What does it mean to be successful?

I recently had coffee with a guy who'd achieved what many Americans would call success. He made a ton of money. He had a five-bedroom, 12,000-square-foot home on a huge lot. But two years ago he lost his job and couldn't find a new one. So he sold his house, his extra cars, his snowblower and lawn mower, and most of his furniture. He moved into a two-bedroom apartment closer to the central city. "It only takes me an hour to clean my whole house!" he told me. And he's never been happier.

At first he felt like a failure. At dinner parties, he noticed that he and his friends were engaged in a cryptic game of one-upmanship. They talked about their "stuff" and doted on each other's baubles. My friend realized he didn't need more stuff. In fact, having and taking care of stuff caused him a lot of anxiety. What he needed was new friends!

As we go through regeneration there will be a growing realization that the way we've always measured success, both individually and as a society, needs to be revised. We need to keep score differently. Start by defining what "success" means to you. And then find friends and invest in experiences that reinforce it.

Principle #4: Nested holons and bottom-up change

A holon is something that is both a whole and a part. For example, you are a human being, a whole system in and of itself. And you are also a part, such as a member of a family. And your family lives in a neighborhood. Your neighborhood is part of a city . . . and so on. I think of these holons as nested within their larger systems, as figure 5 shows.

In open systems, holons self-organize from the bottom up, spontaneously adapting in ways that require cooperation and/or reorganizing between independent parts for mutual benefit.

Let me give you an example.

This past winter, we got a lot of snow in Madison. Our whole neighborhood was having a hard time keeping sidewalks and driveways clear. We'd just get things under control, and another 8 or 17 inches would drop. Or the plow would go by and refill the apron of our driveway with 6 more inches.

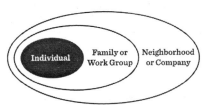

Figure 5: Nested Holons

So a few of us, if we had a little more time, would help our neighbors shovel. I would work on my driveway and sidewalk at about 6 a.m., and if Sandy's sidewalk needed it, I would shovel hers. Sandy noticed, and in the afternoons when she started her snowblower, she'd clear our sidewalk of the day's accumulation.

This neighbor-helping-neighbor ethic caught on and one morning, after it had snowed all night, I woke up and saw that Dean, who lives eight houses away, had blown the snow off the sidewalk from his house all the way to the end of our block!

This snowy example epitomizes the power of nested holons and bottom-up change: each individual holon (person or family) did her part, and soon the other holons were working together to help each other, and eventually the whole block was helping.

The power of bottom-up organization and adaptation is well known. The American Revolution. The fall of the Berlin Wall. The Arab Spring. You often hear this quote by anthropologist Margaret Mead: "A small group of thoughtful people could change the world. Indeed, it's the only thing that ever has."

America's regeneration will feature a lot of nested holons, all reorganizing and adapting to changing conditions. Crowdfunding and locavesting are grassroots movements to move our money off Wall Street (a system that no longer works for most Americans) to Main Street, to put our money in local businesses and entrepreneurs we see every day.

The modern Tea Party started as a 120-person political rally in Seattle. It has become an important modern-day adaptation of the GOP.

Bottom-up adaptations like these often grow and disrupt established systems. And established systems don't like them. They don't know what to do with them, so they often work to quash or limit them. But bottom-up change, like hurricanes that bring oxygen to the ocean's dead zones, are an open system's natural response to stasis.

Here are two ways to put the power of the holon to work:

****

Start where you are.

Go where your energy is.

****

If you want to impact the country, you don't have to be an expert on Medicare or immigration. Simply start where you are, and go where your energy is.

All of us have things we're passionate about. Maybe it's biking to work, or closing the achievement gap. Don't overcomplicate things; just choose. Then get involved. Make friends with others who share your passion, and reach out to other holons that care, too.

It really doesn't matter where you start, but you have to start somewhere.

****

Practice active hope.

****

The challenges facing America are more complicated, and in some cases more dire, than many realize. So you and I need to be very careful about choosing our attitude. I choose "active hope," a term I first heard from ecologist and Buddhist scholar Joanna Macy.

Yes, things are a mess. No, we can't know what the future holds. But between the mess and the future, I choose to believe that I can make a difference and work for that change. I may be only one, but I *am* one.

★★★★

So we're nearly at the end of our time together. And you may be wondering, "How will we know when winter has ended and spring is here?"

It won't flash like a weather alert on your desktop. There won't be a parade. As in other springs, things will thaw, eventually.

One of the most telling signs will be when America moves from "me-mind" toward "we-mind" and from fear toward hope.

In figure 6, I have plotted the emotional tone of America's seasons, between "me" and "we" and between hope and fear.

Figure 6: Hope v. Fear, Me v. We

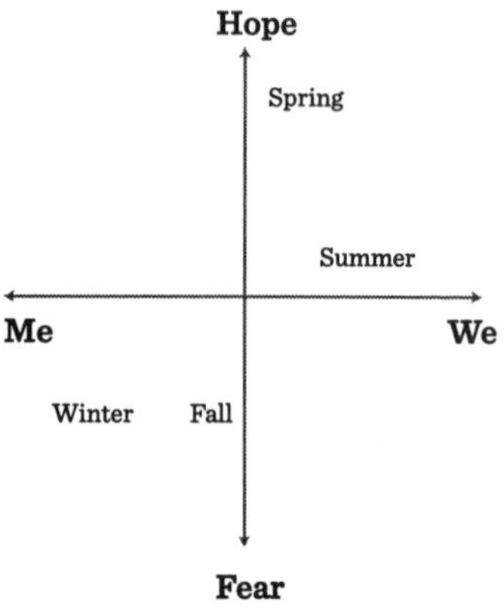

Hope

Spring

Summer

Me   **We**

Winter   Fall

Fear

As we move from winter to spring, you'll sense the tone moving away from selfishness and toward the common good, away from fear and toward hope.

Our leaders will transition from being divisive skeptics to pragmatic collaborators. The emphasis on "Whose idea is it?" will be replaced with "Will this work?" And Americans will, once again, feel that our best days are ahead of us.

In studying America, I sense the in-breath (spring and summer) followed by the out-breath (fall and winter.) Spring and summer are expansions; fall and winter are contractions. The rhythm is always there, keeping time.

Here's to you. Here's to all of us. Here's to regeneration and the promise of making America work better for more people.

The Great Turning
Christine Fry [55]

You've asked me to tell you of the Great Turning
Of how we saved the world from disaster.
The answer is both simple and complex.
We turned.

For hundreds of years we had turned away as life on earth grew more precarious
We turned away from the homeless men on the streets, the stench from the river,
The children orphaned in Iraq, the mothers dying of AIDS in Africa

We turned away because that was what we had been taught.
To turn away, from our pain, from the hurt in another's eyes,
From the drunken father, from the friend betrayed.

Always we were told, in actions louder than words, to turn away, turn away.
And so we became a lonely people caught up in a world
Moving too quickly, too mindlessly toward its own demise.

Until it seemed as if there was no safe space to turn.
No place, inside or out, that did not remind us of fear or terror, despair and loss, anger and grief.

Yet, on one of those days, someone did turn.
Turned to face the pain.

---

55   Christine Fry, "The Great Turning", accessed online June 30, 2012, www.joan-namacy.net/poemsilove/workshop-poems/122-thegreatturning.html

Turned to face the stranger.

Turned to look at the smoldering world and the hatred seething in too many eyes.

Turned to face himself, herself.

And then another turned.

And another. And another.

And as they wept, they took each other's hands.

Until whole groups of people were turning.

Young and old, gay and straight.

People of all colours, all nations, all religions.

Turning not only to the pain and hurt but to beauty, gratitude and love.

Turning to one another with forgiveness and a longing for peace in their hearts.

At first, the turning made people dizzy, even silly.

There were people standing to the side, gawking, criticizing, trying to knock the turners down.

But the people turning kept getting up, kept helping one another to their feet.

Their laughter and kindness brought others into the turning circle

Until even the nay-sayers began to smile and sway.

As the people turned, they began to spin

Reweaving the web of life, mending the shocking tears,

Knitting it back together with the colours of the earth,

Sewing on tiny mirrors so the beauty of each person, each creature, each plant, each life.

Might be seen and respected.

And as the people turned, as they spun like the earth through the universe,

The web wrapped around them like a soft baby blanket

Making it clear all were loved, nothing separate.

As this love reached into every crack and crevice, the people began to wake and wonder,

To breath and give thanks,

To celebrate together.

And so the world was saved, but only as long as you, too, sweet one,

remember to turn.

GRATITUDES

Books don't just happen.

It takes a whole village. That means Village People. These amazing folks crowdfunded this book's first printing. They are my Kickstarter Superheroes, listed below in order of their pledges:

Jan Loiselle

Stephanie Ricketts

Gary Molz

Leslie Ann Howard

Jocelyn Fuller

Jamey Coughlin

Popamatic Studios

Melinda Guillemette

Scott Neils

Charlie Grantham

L. Schreiber

Trey Schwab

Jessie Lerner

J. Kevin Cooper

Penn Engebose

Doug Eno

Drew Pollick

Vickie Moul

Dennis Sterling

Barbara Johnson

Marsha Sheahan

Sonia Kubica

Mike Piggott

Drew & Angela Conrad

Steve Horne

Jason Tennenhouse

Art Kuesel

Tricia Duncan

David Boyer & Joan Phillip

Charles W. Shook

Michelle A. Behnke

Diane Ballweg

Peter Kageyama

Cyd Strickland

Risa Lavine, CohnReznick

Turina Bakken, Madison College

Michael Ritter

Kendra Kinnison

Lauren Rutlin

Beth L. Weckmueller

Sue Gleason

Rodger Ricketts

Jane Boutelle

Peter Moorhouse

George Hofheimer

Jan Eddy

Penny & Phil Molina

Okaybro

Adrian Reif

Amy Soyck

Sam Davidson

Dan Harbeke

Leitschuh Leadership Consulting

Kristin Bakke

Julie Kay Wood

Jan Stranz

Matthew Dunn

RMHC of the Ozarks, Inc.

Kevin Turco

Janet Hartung Renfert

Lane Gorman Trubitt, PLLC

Derek House

Lynette Marling

Lori Woods

Susan Hodkinson

Ray Leach

Scott Harrington

Brian B. Sanderson

Arnaud BASSON

Runzheimer International

Ronald Rauch

Jennifer Smith, MadHIP, LLC

Neil Heinen

Aaron Olver

Nathan Eisner

Jan Mowbray

Sarah White

John Osborne

Alnisa Allgood

Lisa Bayne

Jill M. Lemke

Kevin Straka

Fazio, Mannuzza, Roche, Tankel, LaPilusa

Donna Dittman Hale

Emily Bradley

Jan Allen

Danville Pittsylvania County Chamber of Commerce

Kenneth E. Baggett

Alexis and Lance

Lisa Hanlon

Brian L. Joiner

Donna Gould

Kirsten Case

Leslie Shoemaker

Debra Helwig

Stephen C. Warner

Darcy Kobinsky

Thomas Callam

Brennan Nardi

Jane Coleman

Red Dog Consulting

Pacha

Cynthia Milota

Maureen Costello

Erin Stephenson

Gary S. Shamis

Theresa Hilinski

Toni Sikes

Dennis J. Brieske

Rick Baker

Martha & Dan Larson

Lyndon Clemens

Beth Churchill

Ellen Brothers

Christy Price

Elizabeth Donley

Jaime Leick

Steve Gilbert, Paris Economic Development Corporation

Andy Armanino

Anonymous

Columbia Opportunity Resource

Mark Webster

Dianna Gaebler

David A. Gust

Bob Lazard

Stephen E. Schmid

Marc Eisen

M. Sebastian Comella

Matthew Vanderhorst

Linda Harris

The AsianCajuns

Meredith M. Roark

Alison Ortowski

Karen Windon

Carol Toussaint

Clay Pearson

Garth Sherwin

Katy Simon

Tom Bonfield

Jenna Weber, CONNECT Madison

Daniel Mick, West Hollywood City Hall

Jeremy Lloyd O'Brien

J. Michael Munger

Peggy Merriss, City of Decatur, Georgia

Jenna Boozer

Karen Thoreson

Dan Kennelly

Julie M. Anding

Stacy Phillips Leaming

Jessica Lucas

Josie Osborne and Kim Cosier

Lorenzo Gomez III

Linda Langston

The Kerrigans

Michelle Golden

MiddletonRaines + Zapata LLP

Rita Keller

Lorie Vincent

Ethan Jones

Amanda McGhee

Lisa Benson

Dave Lawrence, Arts Council of Indianapolis

Pierre Uteschill

Kenneth Guidry

Ace Yakey

Brad Hurt

Gale Crosley

Ardyth Richmond

Carol Misner & Ann Huckstep

Lance & Aubrey Patterson

Michele DeWitt

Energy Consulting Network

Renee Moe

Arlene Gavin

Anne Shudy Palmer

Jane Shudy

Carl Weber

Londa Dewey

Jeb Banner

Deidre Myers

David J. Anderson

Kevin Little

Kraig Rodenbeck

Marsha Lindsay

L R Portz

Hanh M. Le

Matthew J. Wise

Richard Biever

Rick Solomon

Brent Starck

Mona Johnson

Cole Carley Communications

Christine Harris

CC Mullen

Dacia Gonzales

Heidi Brundage

Gregg Mandsager

Kathy Kessler

Jim McNulty, Oak Bank

Martha Sullivan

Jackson C. Tuttle

Dave & Virginia Havlovitz

John W. Busey II

Kathy Armstrong

Holden Kellerhals

Amy Lynch

Deidre A. Fountain

GIS Planning Inc.

Tom Stellman

Heather Marie Hunt

Micheal L. Miller

Ben Klepzig

Karen J. Lane

Dace Koenigsknecht

Heather Denker

Fred J. Bauters

Amber Fischvogt

Joan E. Fuller

Jon Sandbrook & Kristin Joiner

Good For Business

Sheryl Wohlford

Paul Kaspszak

John Warren

Jim Hawkins

EZ Office Products

Kevin J. Gienger

Claudia Iverson

Paula Lutz

Mary Hans

Scott Niels

Sandra Sydnor

Kay Plantes

Heather Rogge

Donna Cox

Nancy Wilkinson

Mark Shannon

Teresa Hopke

Rick Grover

Boomer Consulting

Lyn Menne

Jan Mowbray

Jeremy O'Brien

Prime Global

PERSONAL NOTES OF THANKS

I wrote this book in the margins of my life. To create margins, I would set my alarm for 4 a.m. to write before the whole Ryan Ranch woke up. One morning after I'd hit snooze, my sweetheart Marti Ryan rolled over in bed, looked me square in my sleepy face and said, "The book isn't going to write itself." Then she got up and brewed me a cup of coffee. I love having a partner who kicks my butt sometimes.

Speaking of butt kicking, my editor Brennan Nardi is a whiz at walking this tightrope: getting better work out of me without crushing my spirit. Best yet, Brennan—who has been my longtime editor at *Madison Magazine*—agreed to edit this book "because we're friends." Due to her kindness and skill, we still are. Thanks, Bren.

Barbara Walsh proofread this tome, proving once and for all the value of someone who really knows what they're doing with grammar. And the super-talented Daniella Echeverria, who laid out the entire book, made graphs and charts on the fly, and did it all quickly and coolly. Twice.

Books with cool covers sell better. Thanks to artist Dave Taylor for designing *ReGENERATION's* gorgeous cover, key illustrations, and its overall look and feel. And these days, your book needs a trailer, a little movie to announce it to the world. Thanks to Rob Sax at Popamatic Studios, who produced our trailer and connected me with JJ, whose video genius (and musical selection) made the trailer come to life. Thanks, guys, for believing in this project.

Finally, to all of my friends, family, and clients who asked for two years, "Is the book done?" I am happy to finally share *ReGENERATION* with you.